Marbling

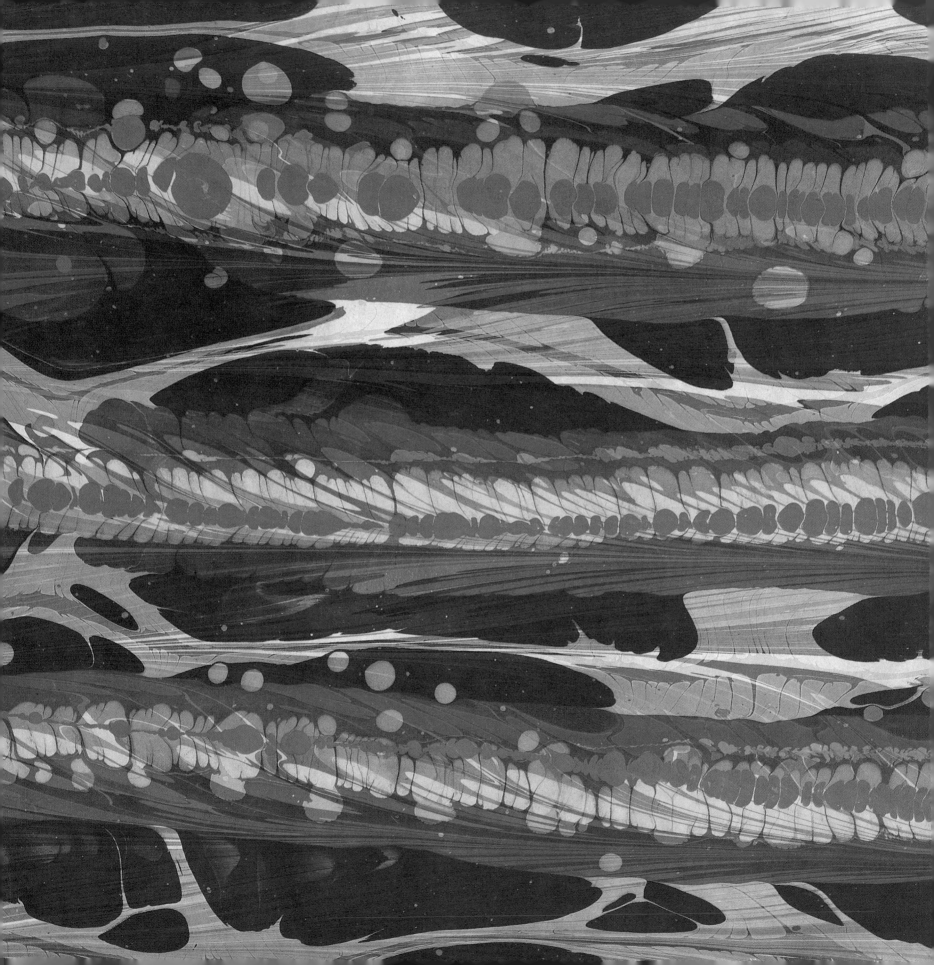

Marbling

A Complete Guide to Creating
Beautiful Patterned Papers and Fabrics

Diane Vogel Maurer

with Paul Maurer

FRIEDMAN/FAIRFAX
PUBLISHERS

A FRIEDMAN/FAIRFAX BOOK

© 1994 by Michael Friedman Publishing Group, Inc.

Library of Congress Cataloging-in-Publication Data

Maurer, Diane Vogel.
    Marbling / Diane Vogel Maurer with Paul Maurer.
        p.   cm.
    Includes bibliographical references (p.   ) and index.
    ISBN 1-56799-113-0
    1. Textile printing.   2. Marbling.   3. Marbled papers.
    I. Maurer, Paul.   II. Title.
    TT852.M38   1994
    745.7--dc20   94-7779
                                                                CIP

Editor: Melissa Schwarz
Art Director: Jeff Batzli
Designer: Susan Livingston
Photography Editor: Christopher Bain

All illustrations © Madeline Sorel
All photography © Bruce McCandless, except as noted below
© Michael Grand: pages 13, 17, 19, 22, 38, 39, 40, 49, 91, 97, 101, 102, 103b, 105
© Free Library of Philadelphia, Rare Book Dept: page 14
Courtesy of the artists: pages 77, 90, 92a, 93b, 95b

The illustration on page 15 is from A Diderot Pictorial Encyclopedia of Trades and Industry, ed. by Charles C. Gillespie, Dover Publication, 1959.

Typeset by The Interface Group
Printed and bound in China by L.Rex Printing Company Limited

For bulk purchases and special sales, please contact:
Friedman/Fairfax Publishers
15 West 26th Street
New York, NY 10010
212/685-6610 FAX 212/685-1307

Dedication

To Ann and John Vogel and to Jane and Paul Maurer who supported the arts and the artists.

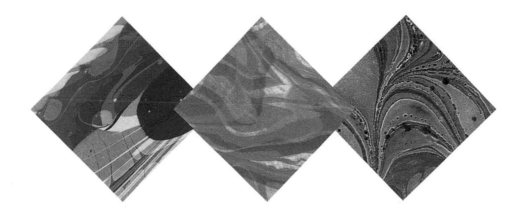

Acknowledgments

I'm indebted to those artists whose exceptional work helped illustrate this book; to Phoebe Easton, marbling historian; and to Faith Harrison, Iris Nevins, and Don Guyot whose marbling and teaching helped foster an interest in the craft. I'm grateful to Jerusha Grosh for her wise counsel and for taking on much of the Hand Marbled Papers business so that I'd have time to write, and to Jennifer Philippoff Tosh whose personal and professional support has always helped sustain me. Thanks, also, to my marbling partner Paul, whose oil-marbling expertise and renegade approach to marbling inspired me and helped shape this book. Finally, my appreciation goes to Melissa Schwarz whose excitement about MARBLING, faithfulness to the manuscript, and light-hearted approach to editing it made working with the Michael Friedman Group such a pleasure.

Contents

"Mauve Forest," a watercolor-marbled paper by
Diane Vogel Maurer.

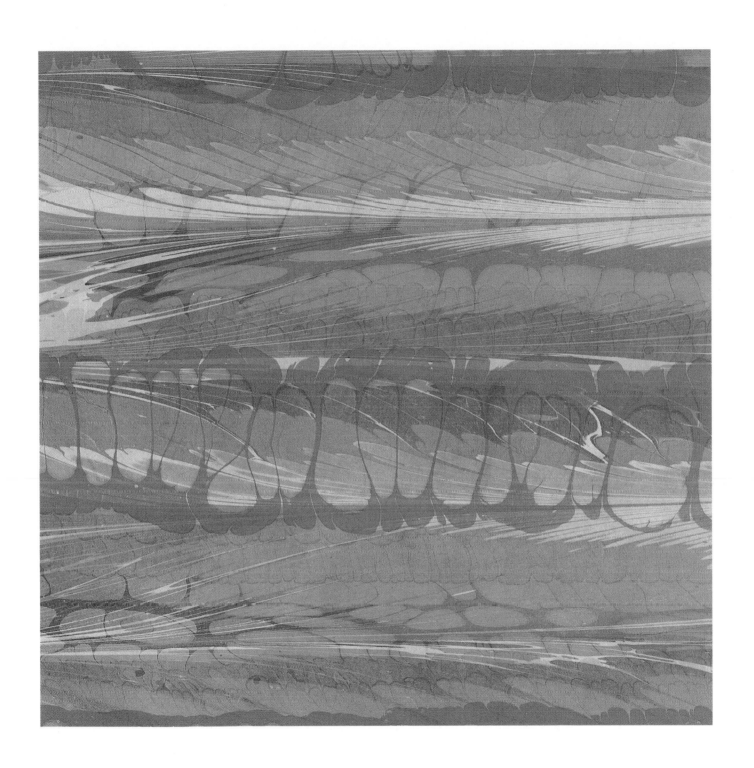

Preface

I NEVER MEANT TO BECOME A MARBLER. IN FACT, I MADE A CONSCIOUS DECISION
to avoid the craft when my partner Paul's interest in it was rekindled several
years ago. I was already dividing my time between writing and weaving, having just
completed my book *Fiber Arts*, and didn't want to further scatter my
energies. When I repeatedly heard Paul's workshop students complain about trying
to learn marbling from sketchy magazine articles, however, all that
changed. I decided to get involved with marbling—from a distance. I put aside
some children's stories I was working on and began a new
book—about watercolor marbling.  Paul and other marblers did their
best to impart their expertise, but the manuscript still had a tentative
sound to it that I couldn't resolve. I wanted to write clearly, without a lot of footnotes

A detail of "Sherbet Flame," a watercolor-marbled paper by
Diane Vogel Maurer.

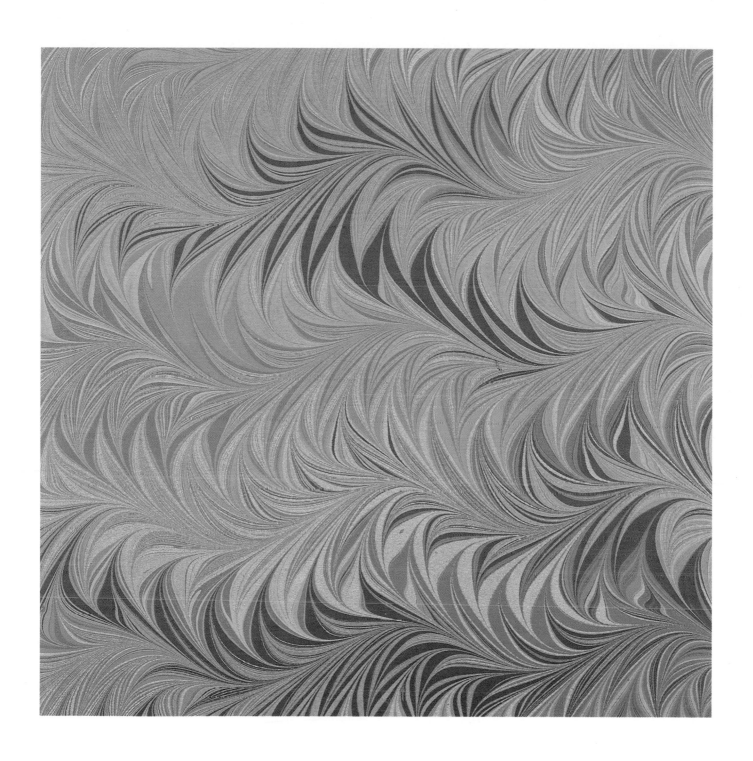

about how to modify marbling paints and size to allow for changes in
temperature, pattern definition, impending mold, or a visit from the ornery marbling
muse I kept hearing about. The muse, it became clear, was a kind of
marbling scapegoat, held responsible for sudden dust spots, sinking color, or
anything else without logical explanation. ❧ It seemed the only way
to clarify my questions was to roll up my sleeves and gain some first-hand
knowledge. Initially I created bold patterns with a palette of primary
colors. I wasn't really marbling—just trying to get a feel for the brushes and whisks
so I could write about them. Then, one fateful evening when I was too
tired to act the professional, I began to play at the marbling tray. First I attempted
to take the scream out of the colors by adding white or black paint to
them. Then I mixed colors with one another until I was surrounded by bottles
and jars of every conceivable hue. As I began to apply and pattern the
colors, I found myself completely captivated! The delicate tonal changes
I'd prized in my fiberwork, and the subtlety I'd sought in my writing,
were apparent in this new and irresistible medium—marbling. I must have
produced forty pastel sheets in a row, I was so excited by the patterns
that appeared as the fine nonpareil combs slid through the warp of
colors. ❧ I continued marbling, and by the time my booklet
An Introduction to Carrageenan and Watercolor Marbling was published in
1984, I was an accomplished practitioner of the craft. ❧ I loved working with
lots of colors and rarely repeating designs, and eventually I amassed such an
overflowing stack of favorites that I began offering them for sale to craft galleries

and museum shops. At one gallery owner's urging, I started to produce
a line of marbled notecards and simple handbound books, often with storybook
interiors. Designing was almost as rewarding as marbling, I learned, and soon
the line of marbled merchandise grew to include picture frames, folios,
and jewelry. To balance the craft aspect of the work (much of which
was now in the hands of two assistants), I began to exhibit marbled paintings and
collages in galleries. Solo shows followed, and they in turn led to invitations
to demonstrate marbling throughout the country. Demonstrations
often led to workshop requests, and from time to time I found myself
teaching watercolor marbling and simple bookbinding courses. It was during a
course at Penland in 1989 that I realized the time had come for a book
like *Marbling*. It has felt good to be writing again, but the loom, I'll admit,
stands covered with dust. I never throw the weaving shuttle anymore;
instead, I throw marbled patterns—and a minor tantrum now and then when the
infamous muse I was warned about some eight years ago pays a visit
while I'm doing detailed work. She'll call on you, too, one day, and her visit will
be a sure sign that you've earned the right to call yourself a marbler.
I think that, rather than an adversary, she's really the spirit of adventure in
disguise, a reminder to relinquish control sometimes, to let the
medium lead you into the mysterious, uncharted realm that divides
the marbling craft from the marbling art.

Diane Vogel Maurer

Chapter One
A Brief History of Marbling

THE ORIGINS AND EARLY DEVELOPMENT OF MARBLING ARE SOMEWHAT OBSCURE, but it is known to have been practiced in Japan, and possibly in China, as early as the twelfth century. Early marbling, called suminagashi, or ink floating, involved floating colors on water to produce delicate swirled patterns which were then picked up on absorbent papers. According to Japanese legend, knowledge of the marbling process was a divine gift to a man known as "Jiyemon Hiroba" to reward him for his devotion at the Katsuga Shrine. Historians, however, suggest that an ancient Japanese game contained the germ of the idea of marbling, and that Hiroba probably expanded on the idea.

Many early nineteenth-century books were printed with original watercolor-marbled endpapers and edges.

A favorite pastime in the twelfth-century royal court was to decorate paper with sumi-ink drawings and then immerse the paper in water. Once the paper was submerged, the inks would float to the surface of the water and produce a fleeting, yet entertaining, image. Whether credit for the idea of marbling is due to the gods or to Hiroba's ability to take game playing a step further, it appears that Hiroba was one of the first to realize that paper could be applied to floating ink to capture and preserve an image.

Another type of marbling, known as Ebru, or cloud art, was evident in Turkey and Persia in the fifteenth century. Instead of floating colors on water, the Persians are believed to have added various mucilaginous materials to water to form a thickened "size," similar to the liquid medium used by Western marblers today. This development gave the marbler more control over color movement and allowed him to create combed patterns in addition to flowing designs. Oil colors and gouache colors were used instead of inks, and they, too, afforded greater mastery of the medium. Work from this period survives to show that in addition to being used on miniatures and calligraphy, marbling was used to create fine borders on manuscripts and to create pictures with silhouetted figures cut from marbled paper.

This early-seventeenth-century ink sketch from the Jahangir School is called "A Fight Between an Elephant Rider and a Man on Horseback." The border and the main body of the sketch are marbled in various colors and are exactly alike. The background is marbled in gray and white.

The sixteenth-century English philosopher Sir Francis Bacon was impressed by the Turkish marbling he saw during his travels. He helped foster an interest in marbling by recounting the following in *Sylva Sylvarum* (1627):

> The Turks have a pretty art of chamoletting of paper which is not with us in use. They take divers oyled colors and put them severally in drops upon the water and stir the water lightly and then wet their paper (being of some thickness) with it and the paper will be waved and veined like chamolet or marble.

Knowledge of the craft spread slowly along the trade routes to Europe, but, by the seventeenth century, France, England, Germany, Holland, and Italy had been introduced to marbled papers. Few people knew how to create the papers, however, and the enthusiasm of those who had witnessed the marbling process did little to make up for their lack of technical knowledge. Marblers proficient in the craft were reluctant to share their knowledge and strictly maintained the shroud of mystery that prevailed over the new art.

A few master marblers, using secret techniques and "magic" formulas, created and named specific patterns, such as French Curl, Old Dutch, and Stormont. As demand for marbled papers grew, master marblers organized guilds and workshops, and they employed apprentices to help with production. But much of the work was accomplished secretly behind wooden partitions, and masters were careful to teach only a few aspects of the craft to each worker, to prevent any of their apprentices from learning enough to establish himself as a competitor.

English bookbinders were eager to use the patterned papers in their bindings, but they knew little about the craft. During the 1600s, they were forced to import work being produced in Holland and Germany. To circumvent having to pay excessive duties, the crafty Dutch often shipped their marbled papers to the binders by using them as wrappings for toys being exported to England. The unfortunate English binders, whose questions about the marbling process went unanswered, were obligated to press some very wrinkled specimens before they could use them as endpapers for their books.

Many of the procedures used in this seventeenth-century marbling shop are still practiced by modern day marblers. Electric blenders, of course, have made preparing the size less tedious, and commercially-made marbling paints and inks have rendered grinding pigments unnecessary.

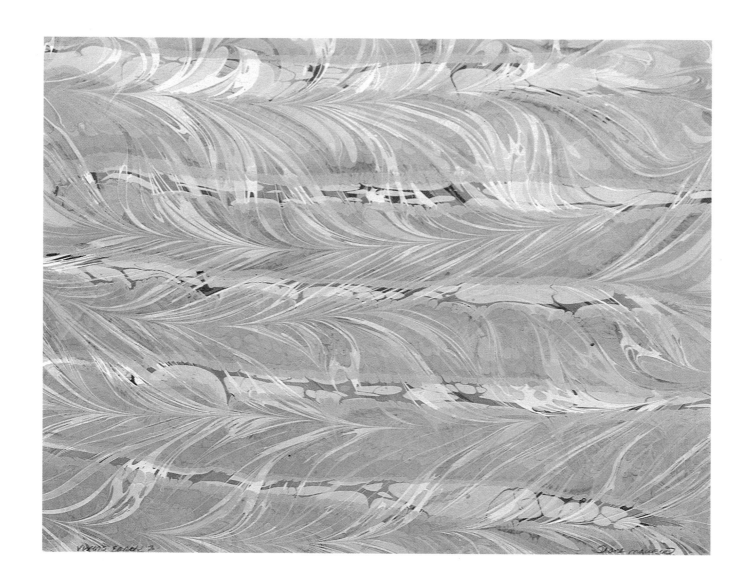

It wasn't until 1853 that detailed and precise instructions for making marbled paper were publicly revealed. That year, the English master Charles Woolnough divulged the entire process in his book *The Art of Marbling.* The majority of marblers were outraged that the secrets of the trade had been disclosed in textbook form and made readily available. Woolnough, however, was confident of his own mastery of the craft and unconcerned about the competition his book might create. James Sumner, Woolnough's chief rival, was apparently of a similar mind. The following year, Sumner published *Mysterious Marbler, or the Mystery Unfolded: Shewing How Every Bookbinder May Become a Marbler.*

Woolnough's book reached American binders in a rather curious fashion in 1856, when James B. Nicholson published *A Manual of Bookbinding,* in Philadelphia. The work contained a section on marbling with complete instructions—all borrowed from Woolnough's *The Art of Marbling.* But Woolnough's writing, as well as his marbling, was able to withstand the competition, and his work was considered the leading text on the craft until 1885, when Joseph Halfer, of Budapest, published his famous book, *Die Fortschritte der Marmorierkunst.*

Halfer's work, which was translated into several languages and published in America in 1894 as *The Progress of the Marbling Art,* simplified and redefined the marbling process, and accelerated the growth of enthusiasm for and practice of marbling in Europe and America.

Unfortunately, by the time handbinders were furnished with a working guide to help them produce marbled papers, book production had changed. Binding machines had come into use, and production volume took precedence over craftsmanship. Handbinders and paper marblers found themselves in little demand. When it was no longer economically feasible to practice marbling, the number of devotees to the craft rapidly declined, and for many years marbling lingered only as an obscure book art.

More recently, with the renewed interest in calligraphy, book arts, and crafts, an interest in marbling has been revived, as well. The twentieth century has shown marbling to be suited to many applications, both in its traditional patterned form and as an expressive design medium. Graphic artists are now using marbling in conjunction with limited edition printing, drawing, and calligraphy, and as a means of creating monoprints. Textile artists are producing marbled wearable art, marbled fabrics and tapestries for interior design, and even for tent environments. Potters, painters, and glass workers are beginning to use marbling in their work, too, while the bookbinders, finally, are having a heyday.

This accordion fold artist's book, entitled "Sticks and Stones" opens to reveal a familiar rhyme from my childhood: "Sticks and Stones may break my bones, but names can never hurt me." Interior "pages" consist of "stone" paper watercolor marbled on a carrageenan size, handmade paper and twigs formed into pockets that hold torn paper on which insults are penned. The original is 9 × 28 inches (22 × 70 cm). (Far left) Monoprint by Diane Vogel Maurer.

Chapter Two
An Overview of Principles, Equipment, and Materials

THE OBJECT OF MARBLING IS TO FLOAT COLORED INKS OR PAINTS ON A LIQUID medium, manipulate the colors into a design, and make a contact print. The intricacy of the print you create will depend upon what type of marbling you practice and whether you want to be involved in the craft as a puddler or as a bona fide marbling enthusiast. Either way, you will surely create some interesting papers and enjoy the experience. The joy of marbling is that beautiful, yet strikingly varied, results can be achieved with both simple and complex working methods. As you go from marbling with water-based colors to marbling with paints that contain an oil base, the images you create will change considerably. You also have the option of controlling designs by changing the type of medium, or "size," upon which your colors are floated and patterned.

A few of the supplies used in watercolor, oil, ink, and sumina-gashi marbling. The choice of tools used to apply and manipulate colors will greatly influence the finished marbled image.

Sizes made from water, from carrageenan (a celluloid extracted from an Irish moss called "carrageen"), from gelatin, and from methyl cellulose each have a different surface tension, making it possible to achieve varying levels of pattern control.

In suminagashi, the original and easiest method of marbling, inks float freely on water, producing meandering lines of color. When applied to a simple size (water that contains a gelatinous substance), inks remain somewhat suspended, allowing you to produce crude combed patterns as well as random designs.

Multiple-image suminagashi prints such as the one above by Jerusha Grosh are made by marbling a sheet of paper, letting it dry, and marbling again over the first image. Intersecting lines of ink create interesting colors and patterns.

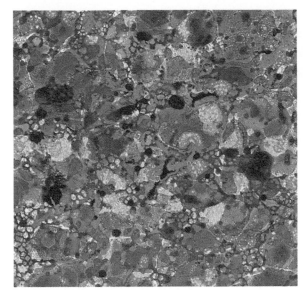

Although drawing inks on a simple size (far left) *can't be combed into detailed patterns, the feathery images created by swirling the colors with a stylus are quite expressive.*

Brilliant oil-color patterns can be made by remarbling a sheet of paper several times, dropping different colors on in layers of spots. We often use gold or silver paint as a final coat to give the rich colors a regal finish.

Six combing steps led to the scallop pattern below. Because watercolor paints can be floated on a carrageenan size, colors remain true throughout the detailed combing process.

With the use of a more sophisticated carrageenan size, watercolors may be manipulated or combed into intricate patterns. Although this marbling procedure is more complex, and the medium more temperamental, serious marblers often find watercolor marbling the most exciting and challenging method to use.

Combing or patterning oil paints on a carrageenan size or a methyl cellulose size produces vivid, yet soft-edged, images, and tiny beads of color will often stipple a print, further enhancing it.

A number of coloring agents, including acrylic paints, are used to marble fabric. The images vary, depending on the size and the colors used.

Specific materials and procedures may differ with each type of marbling, but the following basic equipment is common to all:

The Marbling Workspace

Expect to take up a portion of a room when you're marbling. You'll need adequate table space for the tray and other pieces of equipment, a drying area where lines or drying racks can be set up, and good light. For watercolor marbling, temperature, humidity, dust, and drafts can influence your results, and you'll need extra space for alum-treating the papers. (See Chapter 4 for a detailed discussion of watercolor marbling conditions.)

Marbling Tray

Any pan that's approximately 2″ (5 cm) deep and large enough to accommodate the paper to be marbled will function well. The pan can be made of plastic, metal, or urethaned wood; whatever material you choose should be clean and leakproof. As your interest in marbling increases, you may want to purchase or construct a tray specially designed for marbling, with a drain area. (See instructions in Chapter 9.)

Color Containers

A muffin tin or a watercolor mixing tray works well for holding the inks used in suminagashi and ink marbling, which use a minimum of color. Large jars, or yogurt containers shallow enough to accept an eyedropper yet wide enough to accommodate a whisk, are useful for watercolor and acrylic marbling. For oil-color marbling, using disposable tuna and soup cans cuts down on cleanup time. If you use containers without lids, be sure to cover them when you're finished in order to prevent colors from drying out.

Tools for Dispensing Inks and Paints

Eyedroppers, and floppy natural-bristle brushes such as those used for watercolor painting or lettering, are useful for applying color to the size. The long-haired number 2 or number 4 pointed Oriental brushes are ideal for suminagashi and ink marbling. Larger brushes, broom-straw whisks (see Chapter 4), or 2- to 4-ounce (59-ml to 118-ml) shaker bottles are good for other kinds of marbling. Putting glass beads in the bottom of the shaker bottles helps stir the color. I once used fishing sinkers for this purpose until a conscientious student pointed out that papers made with inks from those bottles probably picked up lead!

Tools for Manipulating Colors

Inks move freely on water. They will readily respond if you blow at them or fan them with a piece of cardboard. A makeshift tool, such as a stylus or a feather, can also be used to get the colors in motion for freestyle ink marbling. In watercolor, oil, or acrylic marbling, tools are the key to creating patterned papers and fabrics. Implements with teeth, such as hair picks and wide-toothed combs, can be used for simple designs. For more detailed work, you'll need special combs and rakes that span the length and width of your marbling tray and that have specific tooth arrangements. (See Chapters 4 and 9.)

The drain area in a specially-designed marbling tray also holds the rinse board in a convenient position. Both beautiful and practical, a urethaned tray like this is a definite advantage for a serious watercolor marbler. Detailed combed papers like my "Sherbet Flame" pictured on the rinse board are difficult to produce in a makeshift tray.

Protective Gloves or Cream

Thin Latex gloves or barrier hand cream from a pharmacy or an art supply store should be worn to protect your hands from the toxic or irritating properties of some of the inks and paints used in marbling.

Skim Board

A narrow skim board, cut slightly shorter than the width of your tray, is used to clean the marbling size. A strip of thin balsa wood 2" (5 cm) wide is ideal, but a piece of a wooden yardstick can also be used.

Skim Strips

Strips of newspaper about 2" (5 cm) wide and a little longer than your skim board are used to remove any ink or paint residue that remains on the size after a print is made. You can cut several strips at once using scissors or a mat knife, but if you have access to a large paper cutter, of course, the work is much easier. Before I purchased my paper cutter, I made annual visits to the studio of a friend, who worked as a framer. On the way there, I'd stop and buy thirteen fat Sunday newspapers—one for my friend, and the rest to be made into a year's supply of skim strips.

Rinsing Equipment

A cookie sheet or a piece of Plexiglas can be used to support the printed sheet during rinsing. If you don't have a sink near your workroom, you'll also need a 1/2-gallon (2-liter) jug for applying the rinse water and a bucket to catch the water. The cover of a specially constructed marbling tray also serves as a rinse board; a hole in the drain section of the tray allows the rinse water to exit into a bucket.

Drying Equipment

PVC pipe, 2" (5 cm) or 3" (7.5 cm) in diameter— a common plumbing supply available at most hardware stores—can be strung on clothesline to make an ideal place to dry papers; they will have good air circulation and will dry relatively wrinkle free, without the crimps thin drying lines create. Wooden or plastic clothes racks can also be used, as long as you space the papers so they don't drip on one another. Whatever you use should be set up away from any heat source, as rapid drying causes papers to buckle.

Keeping Equipment Clean

Unless your equipment has been used for oil-color marbling, it can usually be cleaned with warm water and a scrub brush. Avoid using detergents; they can leave residues that cause havoc with your marbling. If you must use a cleanser, use a mild one, and rinse thoroughly.

Miscellaneous

Other marbling materials, which are detailed in each chapter, include prepared inks and paints, substances that are mixed with water to create the size, and various kinds of paper and fabric to print on. After you've gained some expertise, you may want to try marbling leather, wood, and three-dimensional objects.

Embark on marbling simply at first, using the basic methods described in Chapter 3. When you begin to feel comfortable with the medium, experiment with different types of marbling, bearing in mind that designs are never "wrong," although some are unexpectedly unique. If you remain open to the images that appear in the tray, the medium can guide you through some wonderful adventures.

Chapter Three
Suminagashi and Freestyle Ink Marbling

SUMINAGASHI IS THE SIMPLEST METHOD OF MARBLING, BELIEVED BY MANY TO
be the oldest form of the craft. A few Japanese marblers practice suminagashi
today, using brushes to apply sumi inks and pine resin dispersant to a water size.
Dots of ink and resin are placed on top of one another to form scores of
colored rings, which are then blown into motion to create startling, yet subtle,
designs. You can approximate suminagashi by following this
Japanese method for applying color, or you can create more freestyle
designs by using a less structured color application. Although
little pattern manipulation is possible, due to the watery nature of the
size, it is easy to create lovely marbled images with bright
veins and diffused swirls of color.

Suminagashi overmarbling.

Equipment

A marbling tray, some form of hand protection, color containers, tools for dispensing and manipulating colors, and equipment for skimming, rinsing, and drying (all of which are discussed in Chapter 2) are used for marbling with inks.

Materials

The Size. For this type of marbling, the liquid that the colors float on is water, pure and simple. Or not so pure—any kind of water will do.

Kodak Photo-Flo™ 200. A common darkroom supply, photowetting agent is used in place of pine resin dispersant to control color floating and spreading in suminagashi marbling. Mix a solution of approximately 1 drop of wetting agent to 1 teaspoon (5 ml) of water. The solution functions as a kind of invisible ink, pushing out rings of colored ink on the surface of the water or creating open areas in freestyle designs.

Colors. A number of different types of colors can be used for suminagashi and freestyle marbling. Drawing inks, India ink, and sumi inks in tube, liquid, stick, or cake form, can all be employed. Boku Undo colors also work well, but are harder to find. In general, higher quality paints have better pigmentation and give better results. Dilute colors with distilled water if necessary, but be careful to avoid overdiluting them and losing color intensity. If color drops freely from a loaded brush, it is probably thin enough to work with.

Prepare and use the various colors as follows:

• *Tube Sumi Inks.* Pressing from the bottom of the tube, squeeze some ink into your color container. Gradually mix in water, a few drops at a time, until the ink is of the proper consistency to drop freely from the tip of a brush. A stiff brush or a piece of wood will help to mix the ink well and to dissolve all the paste color. Test the ink by applying it to the water size, and add Photo-Flo™ if necessary.

• *Drawing Inks.* Shellac-type drawing inks, available at art supply stores, can usually be used straight out of the bottle. These inks are available in translucent (dye-like) and opaque (pigmented) forms. Most brands of opaque inks will produce a strong marbled image, but color intensities achieved with translucent inks will vary. Pelican inks, Higgins inks, and airbrush inks produce vivid translucent colors. By investing in small quantities of various brands, you can create a marbling palette of intense, as well as subtle, colors.

Because of their particular chemistries, certain inks dry rapidly when they're exposed to the air, and break up into spots and lines of color when they're patterned. These quick-drying inks can be used alone, or in combination with other types of inks, to produce interesting effects.

Note: Although many commercial inks are labeled 'permanent,' they may not be archivally permanent and may eventually fade when exposed to light. Reds and purples are especially fugitive.

• *Liquid Sumi Inks.* Liquid sumi inks or dyes, such as those made by Boku Undo, will often need a drop or two of Photo-Flo™ to help them spread for marbling. Test by dipping a brush into your color container and then touching the tip of the loaded brush to the surface of the water size. The color should disperse quickly. If the color sinks or doesn't spread as much as you want it to, add your Photo-Flo™, a drop at a time, and mix well before testing again. It's a good idea to work with small amounts of color (perhaps 1 teaspoon [5 ml] at a time), as dipping the brush into the water size and then into the color can sometimes overdilute the color to the point that it must be discarded and replaced.

When working with concentrated sumi ink, add enough water to bring the color to a watery consistency before testing and adding Photo-Flo™.

Although applying several layers of sumi rings for an over-marbled print creates colorful crisscrossing lines, there is also something to be said for a simple, yet graphic single suminagashi print. The amount of dispersant used between applications of color can be varied to focus attention on the meandering rings.

• *India Ink.* India ink, which yields various shades of black, depending upon the brand used, is prepared and used just as liquid sumi inks are.

• *Cake Colors.* Sumi inks can also be purchased in solid cake form, which is available in a number of colors. Each sumi cake is contained in its own ceramic dish. To use cake colors for marbling, mix a small amount of water into the center of the cake, creating a puddle of liquid. Pour off the liquid color into a color container, and test on the water size, adjusting with Photo-Flo™ as necessary.

• *Stick Inks.* Like sumi cakes, stick inks are traditional oriental colors made from a mixture of pigments and hide or fish glues. They are sold in solid form. The making of stick ink is considered an art form in the Orient. People in the West sometimes dislike the process, which requires a bit of time and patience. A shallow slate grinding-dish called a sumi stone (available in art supply stores) is used to abrade the ink stick. Begin by adding about 1 teaspoon (5 ml) or so of water to the deep end of the stone. Then, holding the stick perpendicular to the stone, alternately wet the stick and rub it against the stone in order to gently grind the ink into a solution. Apply moderate pressure and move the stick in a slow circular motion. It's best to leave the stick partially wrapped during the process, as oil from your fingers can damage it. Once you have produced about 1 teaspoon (5 ml) of liquid color, add a drop of Photo-Flo™ and test for marbling.

Papers. Absorbent papers are used for sumina-gashi and freestyle ink marbling. Oriental papers, block printing papers, and unsized handmade papers, all of which are available at art supply stores, are ideal. A few names to look for are Speedball, Unryu, Moriki, and Okawara. Most Western papers contain a sizing that interferes with ink absorption and makes the papers unsuitable for the types of marbling described in this chapter.

Applying and Manipulating Colors

Suminagashi

Several brushes are used to apply the materials for suminagashi marbling: one for each color, and one for applying the diluted Photo-Flo™ dispersant. After testing your colors as explained above, begin with two brushes—one for color and one for dispersant. Barely kiss the center of the water size in your tray with the color-filled brush, releasing a small dot of ink. Then touch the center of the color dot with the tip of the dispersant brush, releasing a bit of photowetting solution. Alternately apply color and dispersant as shown here until a number of concentric rings are formed. Gently blow or fan the inks into a design as shown on the following page.

Early suminagashi masters traditionally held two color brushes in one hand and a dispersant brush in the other as they worked quickly and rhythmically to deposit between fifty and one hundred concentric rings of color on the water size. Their papers were usually marbled with black, or black and indigo, sumi inks, with a focus on subtlety in line and color. Feel free to take liberties with these techniques; Western approaches to suminagashi, using eyedroppers instead of brushes, and various colors with or without dispersants, for example, have produced some striking papers.

A number of color rings are built up in different areas of the tray in preparation for a suminagashi print. When you've gained some expertise, try holding two color brushes in one hand and the dispersant brush in the other hand to apply the inks. Resting your forearms on the sides of the tray may help you apply color quickly and smoothly.

Freestyle Water and Ink

Fill the marbling tray with water and sprinkle the inks with a brush, or gently deposit drops with a dropper, on the surface of the water. Think of yourself as a butterfly rather than as a flyer on a bombing mission—a gentle touch is needed to keep the inks afloat. When you have applied a number of ink droplets, lightly stir or manipulate them with a stylus or a feather to form swirls and patterns of color.

Making the Print. Slowly lay a sheet of paper on the floating inks as shown below, minimizing any movement that might shift the paper and alter the marbled image. Try to make sure that about 1" (2.5 cm) of the paper edge facing you stays dry. Absorbent papers are fragile when wet and will be less likely to tear if you have preserved a dry area you can use to pick them up. A print is made as soon as the paper makes contact with the inks; at that point, thc paper may be slowly peeled off the water (see photo below) and placed image-side up on the rinsc board.

Blowing or fanning the inks helps to get them moving in and around each other to form a design. Absorbant paper captures the moving inks as soon as it contacts them, creating a print.

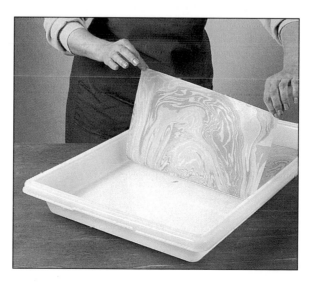

Cleaning the Size. Sometimes the amount of color that remains in the tray after a print has been made is so slight that it won't interfere with the next piece of marbling. After several sheets have been marbled, however, the water size may become muddied, and colors may not disperse properly. It is then necessary to replace the water size in the tray or skim the size to remove any color residue.

To skim, wet the skim board and lay a newspaper skim strip on its surface. Then, starting at the far end of the tray, and holding the board horizontal, submerge one edge of the board about 1/4" (6 mm) below the water-size surface and pull the board toward you over the entire length of the tray as shown. Finally, bring the skim board up and over the near edge of the tray, to remove the unwanted color. Skimming is especially easy to accomplish with a tray that has a drain area. If you're working with a makeshift tray, you may want to place layers of newspaper at the near end of the tray to absorb the excess dripping that occurs during skimming. If necessary, replace the newspaper strip and skim again.

The traditional method of skimming in marbling involves skimming with the board when the size is exceptionally dirty, and skimming 2 or 3 times with a newspaper strip between prints, at other times. When I broke my arm last year and had to find a way to skim one-handed, I found using the board to support the strip an ideal way of working. In the process I discovered that I could clean the size in one action, instead of two or three. What they say about necessity must be true....

During the skimming process, the ends of the newspaper skim strip drag against the sides of the tray preventing a backwash of color from escaping around the edges of the skimboard.

Rinsing and Drying. Some papers will absorb all the color applied and won't require rinsing. Others will show color bleeding or streaking, indicating excess color that should be removed. To rinse, work at a sink or over a basin. Keeping the paper on the rinse board, slowly pour water over the marbled image. Start at the top of the print, just below the dry edge, and work down, continuing to rinse until the color stops running. Then lift the paper slightly and pour water underneath it, as well. On thin papers, excess color deposited on the back of a print will often show through to the front.

Allow the paper to drain for a moment, then carry the rinse board to the drying area, remove the print, and hang it gently.

Pressing Marbled Prints. Absorbent papers won't usually buckle or wrinkle if they dry slowly. Papers that do need pressing can be stacked and weighted with a board or with heavy books. You can also iron marbled sheets by pressing them lightly on their wrong sides with a dry iron set on low heat.

Freestyle Ink Marbling on a Simple Size

The addition of a gelatinous substance to water creates a thickened size for marbling. When inks are applied, they remain suspended in the size instead of floating freely, as they do on plain water. More control is possible this way, and color can be teased into a design or patterned to a limited degree. Some of the procedures followed in freestyle marbling on a simple size are also used in carrageenan marbling (discussed in the next chapter); freestyle marbling can help prepare you for the more complex carrageenan-marbling experience. Working on a simple size is more than just a transition, however; specific design opportunities present themselves in this kind of marbling. A thin size invites Japanese patterning. On a thicker size, sprinkling techniques and simple combing movements are possible. Finally, on a size thickened to an almost-solid state, unusual images can be obtained by drawing into it directly.

Equipment

In addition to the basic marbling equipment discussed previously, you'll need a 1/2-gallon (2-liter) pot for preparing some of the sizes, and a pan of warm water for slowing the gelling process in food-gelatin marbling. The warm-water pan should be large enough to hold both the marbling tray and enough water to surround the tray.

Materials

The Size. The marbled images created with simple sizes will vary depending upon what type of size is used and how gelled or fluid the size is when the print is made. All of the following widely available substances will produce a workable simple size. The recipes are for a 13″ × 20″ (33 cm × 51 cm) tray. Adjust the recipes for larger trays, and change the proportions to create thicker or thinner sizes. Bubbles will form when the size is first poured in the tray and can easily be skimmed off as shown on the following page.

This freestyle ink print shows the typical spot and swirl design created by patterning with a stylus on a thick methyl cellulose size.

• *Methyl Cellulose.* Stir 4 tablespoons (59 ml) of methyl cellulose into 6 pints (3 liters) of cold water until well mixed. Let the mixture stand for about fifteen minutes, stirring occasionally, until the size loses its milky appearance and becomes clear and smooth. Then pour the size into the tray.

• *Psyllium Seed.* Add 6 tablespoons (150 g) of psyllium seed to 2 quarts (2 liters) of boiling water, and stir for several minutes. Then add 2 pints (1 liter) of cold water, stir, and let the mixture stand for several hours. When most of the seeds have settled to the bottom of the pot, pour off the psyllium water into the marbling tray.

• *Liquid Starch.* Use liquid starch straight from the bottle, or mix powdered starch into a solution.

• *Unflavored Food Gelatin.* Dissolve 1 ounce (28 g) of food gelatin in 1 pint (.5 liter) of boiling water. Add 1 pint (.5 liter) of room-temperature water, stir, and pour into the marbling tray. Gelatin sets rapidly as it cools. Place the marbling tray in a pan of warm water to slow the gelling process, or if you prefer, allow the gelatin size to approach a solid state as you marble. Unique images form naturally as the gelling size contorts the colors into patterns.

Papers. Papers used for marbling on a water size (see page 27), are also used on simple sizes.

Color. Most opaque and translucent drawing inks and airbrush inks can be used on simple sizes. The inks will usually spread and float correctly if they are applied with a gentle touch. Because the chemical makeup of different inks varies, however, you may find that certain inks are reluctant to float, while others are so aggressive that they spread too much and cause inks subsequently introduced into the tray to sink. A thickened size makes this problem more likely to occur. Problem inks may be adjusted with Photo-Flo™, as described below, and should be applied in a sequence—warm or light colors first; cool or dark ones last. Pelican, Higgins, Speedball, Badger, Calli, and Rotring inks usually work well. Quick-drying inks that break up when patterned can also be used for their novel effects.

Photowetting Agent. Inks that tend to sink can often be coaxed into performing correctly if undiluted Photo-Flo™ is added to them. Add a drop of dispersant to at least ¹/₃ ounce (10 ml) of ink, mix well, and apply a drop of the adjusted ink to the size. Repeat the procedure until the ink floats. Beware of overadjusting the inks; if they spread too much, they'll lose color density and become almost invisible.

Procedures

Preparing the Size and Colors. Prepare your size and colors following the instructions above.

Applying Colors. Inks can be applied to the size directly from the bottle, using droppers, or delivered by various types of brushes. Applying the colors gently, rather than flinging them down, will help them stay afloat and will minimize excess color deposits in the size. When delivering a single drop of ink with a brush or dropper, barely touch the surface of the size. Sprinkling the size with various colors can be accomplished by lightly shaking them from a soft brush. Drawing your thumb across the bristles of a toothbrush will stipple or spray the size with color.

When working with a methyl cellulose size, the first step (top) is to skim off the bubbles that form on top. Inks that spread excessively like those shown here may sink somewhat when patterned, but the linear effects achieved are often worth it.

On a thin size, the colors tend to pattern themselves in the wake the comb or feather creates, so lifting the print often yields a surprise. Once the print is made, rinsing (**bottom right**) only removes excess color.

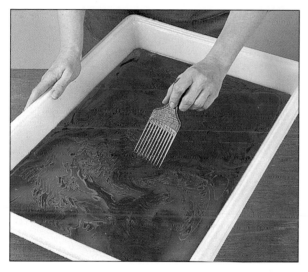

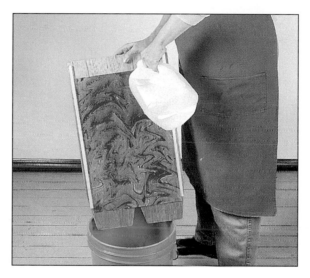

Patterning. Blowing at the inks through a soda straw, or fanning them with a piece of cardboard as shown on page 29, will gently propel them into motion on thinner sizes. Teasing or manipulating the colors with a makeshift stylus, such as a hairpin or a needle, will allow you to draw on sizes of various thicknesses to produce images that range from subtle to more defined. Soft-edged combed designs can be made by drawing a variety of toothed implements through the applied inks. (See photos left and above.)

Making the Print. Lay a sheet of absorbent paper on the surface of the size to make a contact print as shown on page 29, keeping the paper steady so as to accurately transfer the marbled design. You can also shift, slide, or flutter the paper as it's applied to the size; this will alter the image (see pages 86 and 87). When using fragile papers, keep one edge dry for safer, easier handling.

Rinsing, Drying, and Skimming. Rinse the marbled paper as shown above (also see page 30). Remove bits of thick size by gently scraping with a rubber spatula. Hang the print to dry, and skim the size in preparation for the next print (see page 30).

Myriad images can be made by altering the thickness of a simple size. Color, too, can be applied both sparsely or in great quantity, to achieve simplicity or intense drama in a paper.

Troubleshooting

A Particular Color Consistently Sinks.

Because of differences in chemical makeup, some colors are more aggressive, and more likely to spread and float, than others. If a particular ink consistently sinks, it can usually be made more buoyant by adjusting it with a drop or two of undiluted Photo-Flo™. Pour at least ⅓ ounce (10 ml) of ink into a container, and add Photo-Flo™ a drop at a time, mixing well and testing on the size until the ink cooperates.

Various Colors Sink When Other Colors Are Applied.

Most colors will float with each other if you apply them gently. If you happen to be an uncontrollably exuberant person, however, or if you have a strange batch of inks and run into trouble, try this: Apply your inks in a sequence, using warm or light colors (i.e. pinks, yellows, light browns) first, and cool or dark colors (i.e. strong blues, greens, violets) last. The chemistry of cool colors usually makes them more aggressive; if they are applied last, they are less likely to cause other colors to sink.

Color Sinkage and Tray Pollution.

Slight color sinkage is to be expected. If you find that you constantly have to change the water between prints, you're probably being too heavy-handed in your color application.

Color Adherence Problems.

If most of the color runs off as you lift the wet print from the size, you've probably used a non-absorbent paper or one containing too much sizing, which repels the ink. Repeated color bleed usually indicates that more color is being applied than the paper can absorb.

Colors Print Progressively Lighter.

This is a common problem in suminagashi marbling, and it usually occurs when brushes absorb too much water as color is delivered to the water size. Only the tip of the brush should enter the water. Otherwise, excess water picked up by the brush will be transferred to the color, diluting it when the brush is dipped again.

Chapter Four
Watercolor Marbling

THE CARRAGEENAN-AND-WATERCOLOR METHOD IS THE MOST COMPLICATED TYPE of marbling. Materials share a subtle relationship with one another and with the temperature and humidity of the marbling workspace. Papers, colors, and sizes must all be carefully prepared, and attention must be given to a number of details in order to receive optimum results. The medium is temperamental—downright ornery some days, fully cooperative others. Still, most marblers find this the most satisfying medium, as it allows the widest latitude in image making. Watercolors floated on a size made from carrageenan can be combed into finely detailed patterns and teased into crisp fantasy drawings. Although highly sophisticated work requires some experience and an ideal working environment, exciting and varied marbled images can be achieved with a little effort.

A waved pattern, a variation of nonpareil combing.

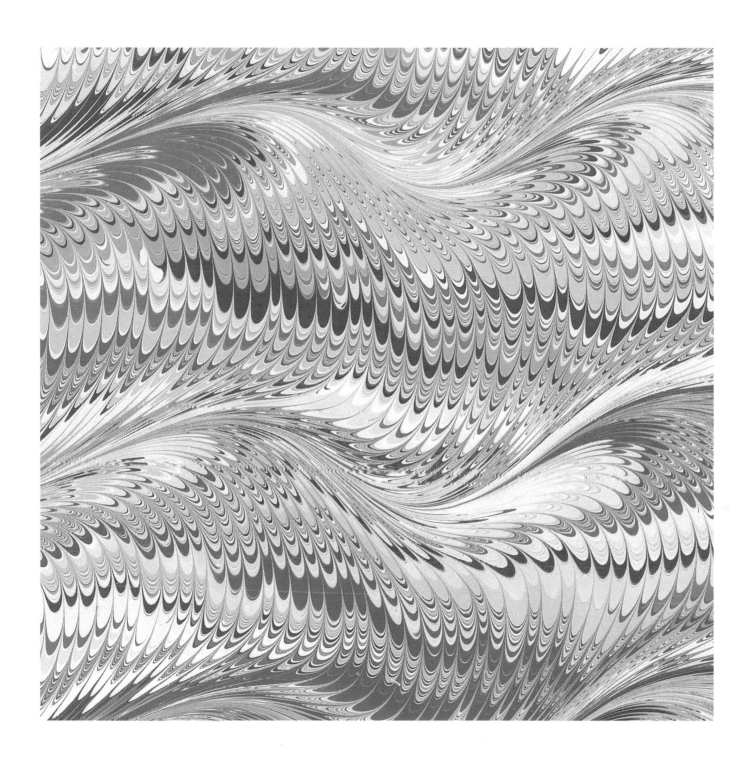

As you explore carrageenan-and-watercolor marbling, you'll learn how to exercise control to produce specific results, and how to surrender control to let the medium guide you through a limitless range of expressive designs.

Equipment

You can purchase specially designed marbling equipment, construct it yourself, or improvise using household items. Instructions for making a simple whisk, rake, and comb are included in this chapter, as these tools take little time to make and are essential to many designs. Detailed instructions for constructing a marbling tray, a rinse board, a skimming board, and combing implements can be found in Chapter 9. Such equipment, although not essential, can add speed, ease, and precision to your marbling efforts.

In addition to a tray, protective gloves or cream, and rinsing, skimming, and drying equipment (all of which is discussed in previous chapters), you will also need the following:

Equipment for Making the Size
- A 1-gallon (4-liter) jug, for dispensing water
- A 5-gallon (19-liter) bucket, for mixing the size
- An electric blender (Carrageen is an edible seaweed and can be mixed using regular kitchen equipment.)

A Humidifier or a Plant Mister. One or the other is needed to increase the level of humidity in the workspace and to keep alum blotters moist.

A Small Tray. A separate tray 8″ × 10″ (20 cm × 25 cm) or larger will be needed for adjusting and testing the colors.

Color Containers and Dispensers. Those suggested on page 22 can also be used for carrageenan-and-watercolor marbling.

Aluming Equipment
- A 1-quart (1-liter) pot, for dissolving the alum (The pot should be reserved for marbling only.)
- A sponge for distributing the alum solution
- 2 large sheets of blotter paper, for enveloping freshly alumed papers
- 2 boards ¹/₂″ (1.3 cm) thick and approximately 12″ (30 cm) wide, for sandwiching the stack of alumed sheets and keeping them flat. Label the edge of one board "alum side up" and the edge of the other, "alum side down."

Pattern-Making Tools. Makeshift tools such as those discussed in previous chapters can be used, or you can make the simple tools described here. Directions for making more sophisticated equipment appear in Chapter 9.

Making a Whisk

The whisk is an ideal tool to use for watercolor marbling. One can be made from natural broom straw, purchased from a marbling supplier, or cut from a household broom. To make a whisk, gather enough broom straw to form a bundle 1″ (2.5 cm) in diameter. Cut the straw to about a 6″ (15 cm) in length, tap it until the ends are even, and bind it with a rubber band. Use either the grassy or the stiff end, as you desire; the size and flair of the whisk, and the thickness and regularity of the straw, help to determine the type of image produced.

Making a Simple Rake

1/4" (.6-cm) thick balsa, pine, foam core, or similar material serves as the base for this simple rake. Cut a piece 1" (2.5 cm) wide and slightly longer than the length of your marbling tray. Slip 2 1/2" (6.4-cm) drapery hooks onto the base material at 1" (2.5-cm) intervals, as shown. Because the rake teeth are set far apart, they can work around the edges of the marbling tray, and the rake can be used vertically as well as horizontally.

Making a Simple Comb

Styrofoam or balsa wood that's 1/2" (1.3 cm) thick makes a good base material for a comb. Cut a strip 1/2" to 3/4" (1.3 cm to 1.9 cm) wide and slightly shorter than the length of your marbling tray. Draw a line lengthwise down the center of the strip, and mark it off in 1/4" (.6-cm) increments in order to help position the comb teeth. Then push 1 3/4" (4.4 cm) T-pins or long dressmaker's pins through the base material at every 1/4" (.6-cm) mark, as shown. (If necessary, run a line of glue or tape over the heads of the pins to keep them stable.) Because the comb teeth are set close together, they won't work around the edges of the tray. To pattern vertically, make a second comb slightly shorter than the width of your tray.

Materials

The Size. Carrageen, also called "Irish seaweed" and "chondus crispus," is used to make the size. Widely used in the food and medicine industries as a binder or thickener, carrageenan, the celluloid extracted from carrageen, forms an ideal marbling medium. It can be purchased from marbling supply houses, and sometimes from health-food stores, in granules, chips, or in powdered form. The no-cook blender variety, available from marbling suppliers, is the most convenient to use.

Distilled Water. Because the quality of tap water varies, and since excessive mineral content can influence the performance of size and colors, it's best to use distilled water for making the size and diluting the colors when you begin watercolor marbling. Later you may want to try marbling with tap water or rainwater to see if you get similar results.

Colors. Various paints and inks can be used on a carrageenan size. The least troublesome are water-based marbling inks and marbling paints, available from marbling supply houses. Some varieties of tube gouache, although difficult to mix properly, can also be used.

Dispersing Agent. Ox gall, which can be purchased from marbling suppliers, is added to watercolor paints to enable them to spread and float on the size. Photo-Flo™ used in water and ink marbling can be used as a substitute for gall.

Papers. Highly absorbent papers, such as most oriental papers and other papers used in water-and-ink marbling, can be used for watercolor marbling and need no aluming. Because the color is absorbed, however, the images achieved have a soft quality to them that might not be suitable for some projects. Most art papers and commercial papers in various cover, text, and bond weights will produce a vivid marbled image if they are alumed prior to marbling. Colored papers are especially interesting to work with. They not only add another color to each marbled sheet, but can expand a limited color palette by providing a base color to alter other colors applied to the sheet. Fine-quality charcoal papers will often enliven a marbled image, but they are somewhat expensive. Personal preference and budget will guide you in choosing papers.

Papers to avoid include newsprint and light-weight construction papers that break down when wet. Highly polished or coated papers may be disappointing, too, as their coatings may repel the alum and produce irregular images. It's best to test a sheet of any specific paper before buying a large quantity for marbling, as paper manufacturers are now coating many sheets with a calcium buffer. The buffer makes papers last longer but causes them to repel marbling color. Check with local printers; they may be able to sell you uncoated stock.

A sampling of paper brands often used by marblers (and uncoated as of this writing) include Canson, Strathmore, Aquabee, Classic Laid, Scott Offset, Hopper, Mohawk, and Carnival.

Note: The permanence of paper is influenced by the type of pulp from which the paper is made—linen, cotton, wood, etc.—and by the chemical additives used in the papermaking process. Papers that last indefinitely and meet high archival standards are usually made from cotton or linen rag and are labeled "acid free" or "neutral pH." When working with these fine papers, care should be taken to avoid contaminating them; use deionized or distilled water for the marbling size. The question of whether or not the alum mordant will cause such papers to fall apart faster is open to debate. Since papers alumed and marbled hundreds of years ago still survive, many marblers tend to believe that mordanting, especially with pure aluminum sulfate, will not seriously decrease paper life.

Alum. Non-absorbent papers must be mordanted, or coated with a solution of alum and water, to enable them to retain a marbled image. Without proper aluming, color won't adhere and winds up deposited in the rinse bucket instead of on the paper. The alums used in marbling, which are available from marbling or fiber-art supply houses, are aluminum sulfate, aluminum potassium sulfate, and aluminum ammonium sulfate. These alums are not the same as that used for pickling purposes.

The Workspace

Although marbling can be practiced in almost any environment, cool (50°–65° F/10°–18° C), humid, clean conditions will help keep problems to a minimum. You'll need good light, but sunlight should not shine directly on the alumed papers or colors, as it tends to dry them out. Sunlight shining on the size can cause variations in surface tension and interfere with color floating. Air-conditioning removes too much moisture from the environment, and the dry air may cause a skin to form on the size.

When working in warm temperatures (up to about 90° F/32° C) you'll have to use a thick size of medium cream consistency. Expect to lose some image sharpness. Higher temperatures cause the size to have less surface tension, which results in your having less control when patterning colors.

Drafts, too, will adversely affect the size and will blow dust particles into the marbling tray. Dust can be a serious problem, as the smallest particle can cause an enlarged, unpatterned spot on marbled papers. Humidity will minimize dust movement and keep the size and papers in good condition. Set up a vaporizer in your workspace, if possible, or mist the air often with a plant sprayer.

Procedures

Making the Size. A recipe for preparing blender carrageenan size, which can be purchased from marbling suppliers in a quantity to fill a 20″ × 30″ × 2″ (51-cm × 76-cm × 5-cm) tray, follows. If you're working with a smaller tray, modify the recipe or freeze the excess size for later use.

Papers in many colors, weights, and textures can be used for various types of marbling.

Blender Size. To complete this recipe you will need about 6 tablespoons (150 g) of powdered no-cook carrageenan and 3 gallons (11.4 liters) of distilled water.

Add enough water to half-fill your blender, and turn the setting to "low." *When the water is in motion*, slowly sprinkle in 1 tablespoon (25 g) of size, and blend for several seconds to dissolve the powder. Add more water, enough to bring the blender to three-quarters full, and blend another minute. Pour this solution into your 5-gallon (19-liter) bucket. Half-fill the blender with water again, and repeat the process until all the carrageenan powder has been mixed with water and deposited in the large bucket. Add enough water to fill the bucket up to the 3-gallon (11.4-liter) measure; this should bring the size to the consistency of milk. Then stir, pour the solution into the marbling tray, and cover it. It's best to let the size age for about twelve hours before using it, as colors adjusted for fresh size may have to be altered when the size matures. Images will be sharper when produced on a mature size, as well.

Skimming the Size. The bubbles which appear in the size as a result of blending should be removed from the tray by skimming the surface of the size with a skimming board as discussed on page 30. Be sure that the skim board is clean to avoid introducing dust into your marbling tray. Cover the tray when it's not in use; even tiny particles of dust can alter your marbled images. Depending upon the temperature of your workspace and the amount of marbling you've done, the size may retain its ability to produce crisp images for several days. After that, the size begins to spoil, and surface tension decreases. Although image clarity will diminish when the size is past its prime, older size can be used for experimental designs.

Use the skimming board and newspaper skim strips to remove the microscopic skin that constantly forms on the size (especially in dry conditions), and to remove any color residue from the size between prints.

Aluming the Paper. Before a sheet of paper can be marbled, it must be treated with an alum-water solution to make it receptive to the marbling colors. Prepare the alum-water mordant by placing 2 tablespoons (50 g) of alum in a pot reserved for this purpose. Add 1 pint (.5 liter) very hot water, and stir until all the alum crystals are dissolved. When the solution is cool enough, place a sponge in the alum solution (wear some sort of hand protection to prevent irritation), wring the sponge out slightly, and wipe the solution onto the paper. Use overlapping strokes, being sure to moisten, but not saturate, the paper; alumed papers must be dry before they can be marbled, and sheets that are too wet will not only take an excessively long time to dry, but they will tend to buckle and wrinkle during the process. Take care, too, that every bit of the paper is alumed—missed areas will show in your marbled patterns.

Lay a piece of blotter paper on top of your board marked "alum side down." As sheets are mordanted, stack them, alum side up, on top of the blotter paper. Cover the top sheet of alumed paper with another piece of blotter paper, and cover the blotter paper with the second aluming board (marked "alum side up"); this arrangement will keep the damp papers from curling and will aid in uniform drying between sheets. When a number of sheets have been alumed (a dozen sheets will be enough for a good marbling session), invert the stack of papers and boards. The paper will now be alum-side-down and ready to print, and the sheets moistened first will be on the top of the stack. If these first papers are dry to the touch and don't have mottled areas, which indicate pockets of moisture, they are dry enough to be marbled.

Note: Alum tends to crystallize when it's exposed to cool temperatures, or when it sits for a number of days. An alum-water solution that has separated can be reconstituted by reheating it.

Preparing Color. Various types of coloring agents can be used for marbling on a carrageenan size, but prepared water-based marbling color is the easiest for the novice to control. It's available in two types: paint and ink. Paint is a complex gouache-type color, highly pigmented and opaque. Ink is a simpler, but carefully mixed, color that can be intense, yet vividly translucent. Some tube gouache also works well but requires more attention for consistently good results.

Protect all colors from freezing, and keep them in tightly closed containers when not in use. Exercise caution when handling colors; a number of pigments used in watercolor paints are toxic. Never eat or smoke if you have color on your hands, and store all marbling supplies out of the reach of children and pets. It's wise to wear gloves or barrier cream to protect your hands (especially from metallic pigments) when preparing colors for marbling.

Prepared Marbling Colors. These colors must be thoroughly mixed, as the pigment readily separates. The proper ratio of ingredients is critical in watercolor marbling. You will have to stir the colors often during marbling to keep the pigments in suspension. Check each color before using it to determine if any has settled or congealed at the bottom of the jar. If it has, pour off the liquid into a clean container and mix the pigment back into a paste. Then gradually add the reserved liquid, stirring thoroughly.

To dilute your colors for marbling, pour a 1" (2.5-cm) depth of mixed stock color into a resealable plastic or glass container. Then add enough distilled water to bring the color to about the consistency of milk. If you're using paint, you can dilute it by up to one hundred percent (for a solution that's half paint, half water) and still maintain considerable opacity. If you're working with ink, add less water to avoid losing color vividness.

Tube gouache. To use these colors, squeeze approximately 2 tablespoons (30 ml) from the tube into your color container. Thoroughly mix the gouache from a paste to a cream by sparingly adding distilled water. Then add enough distilled water to bring the gouache to a medium cream consistency. Because tube gouache sometimes is not well blended within the tube, you may have some problems trying to mix it. If a watery fluid oozes from the tube when you squeeze it, the gouache binder has separated from the pigment. In that case, squeeze out the entire contents of the tube into a container, and thoroughly mix the binder and pigment back together before trying to dilute the gouache. If the color seems lumpy, gritty, or stringy when you squeeze it from the tube, blend it on glass with a mixing knife, or use a mortar and pestle to smooth it out, before continuing.

Unfortunately, because gouache colors are created for watercolor painters, not marblers, the chemistry of some of the paints is incompatible with marbling. The makeup of a particular color can even change from batch to batch, further confusing the novice. Some of the colors in the Windsor Newton Designer Gouache series that usually work are Cadmium Red, Yellow Ochre, Indigo, Lamp Black, and Permanent White. You may want to start with these basic colors and mix others from them.

Metallic Colors. You can create metallic paints by adding mica particles, sold by some papermaking supply houses, to your colors. Usually a teaspoonful (5 ml) of dry particles mixed into color that has been prepared and adjusted will float, spread, and shine quite brilliantly. A mask should be worn when working with mica particles.

Adding Dispersing Agents to Colors. Ox gall or a substitute, such as Photo-Flo™, is added to diluted colors for three reasons: 1) It allows colors to overcome the surface tension of the carrageenan size so that they float and spread instead of sinking. 2) It forms a microscopic wall of fat around each particle of color, thereby preserving the color's identity and allowing different colors to be manipulated into patterns without blending. 3) It reacts with the alum to help bond colors to the paper.

The amount of gall that must be added to marbling colors to make them perform correctly depends upon several variables: the humidity and temperature of the workspace; the thickness, maturity, and temperature of the size; and, most of all, the potency of the gall. Avoid using painter's gall, which is sold in art supply stores, as it is usually too diluted for marbling. Marbling supply houses can furnish you with a strong solution of gall, although potency may vary from bottle to bottle. A few drops of a good aged gall mixed into your paint is usually enough to make a color bouyant. If you're using a weaker gall, you may have to add several times that amount to achieve the same results. Try to avoid using weak gall if you intend to do fine-combed papers. Because of its fatty nature, gall doesn't completely mix with color, and excessive amounts of gall tend to collect on the size and interfere with detailed patterning.

Preparing Colors. To avoid muddying the tray, the novice marbler should adjust colors in a separate pan of size. An 8″ × 10″ (20-cm × 25-cm) baking pan will be large enough to approximate the surface tension in the actual marbling tray. Eventually you will be able to gauge gall requirements and adjust the colors quickly in a corner of the marbling tray, but initially you have to do some patient experimenting. Problems can be minimized if, before you begin to test the color, you make sure that your size has been thoroughly skimmed and that it's about the same temperature as your color.

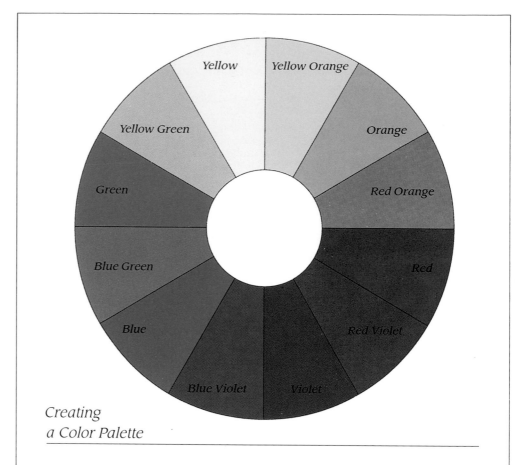

Creating a Color Palette

An extensive color palette can be obtained by color mixing. Twelve hues can be created using the primary colors: red, yellow, and blue.

Primary, secondary, and tertiary colors can be further altered by tinting with white or shading with black.

Colors are tested by applying them to a freshly skimmed size, using a whisk or an eyedropper. A smaller droplet of color is delivered from a whisk than from an eyedropper, so colors tend to float more readily and require less gall when they are tapped from a whisk. If you plan to marble patterns that don't require the use of a dropper or a brush, you can adjust colors for whisk application. Many patterns require that color be delivered by various types of applicators, however, so it's best to spend the extra time making colors buoyant enough for any type of delivery.

A single pass with a rake printed over a previously marbled nonpareil design created this overmarbled print. The color choice for the second layer in a multiple-image piece should be translucent or applied sparingly enough to allow the first pattern to show through.

Adjusting and Testing Colors. Using a separate testing tray and an eyedropper, gently apply stirred, diluted color to the size surface. A drop of color will usually form a small bead and sink. If this happens, skim off the test area, add 1 drop of gall to the color, *stir well*, and test the color again. Continue adding gall in increments of 1 or 2 drops, mixing and applying color to the size until it floats with a minimum of sinkage. Ideally each drop of color should spread to form a circle 2″ to 4″ (5 cm to 10 cm) wide that stays afloat without contracting. Fine tuning will come with experience. Watch for the problems illustrated in the Troubleshooting Chart on page 62, they can influence the performance of your colors and the crispness of the marbled images.

When each of the colors is adjusted to float and spread individually, you should begin to test a number of colors together in the tray. Add more gall to a color if it sinks when others are applied. Try introducing colors into the tray in several sequences until they are all adjusted to stay afloat simultaneously. It will be difficult for novices to completely eliminate color sinkage. For your initial marbling efforts, if most of the colors float, go ahead and create a pattern and make the print.

Making Gall Water. When the colors have been tested, and you've determined how much gall is needed to keep them afloat, you can similarly adjust distilled water to use as "invisible color." For instance, if you used 3 drops of gall to adjust ¹/₂ cup (118 ml) of diluted marbling color, you can add 3 drops of gall to ¹/₂ cup (118 ml) of water to produce gall water. When it's applied to colors on the size, gall water spreads and creates clear areas for design use. It can also be combed to allow colored paper to show through a marbled pattern and integrate with other colors applied. Finally, when gall water is applied *over* other colors, it compresses them and intensifies their pigmentation.

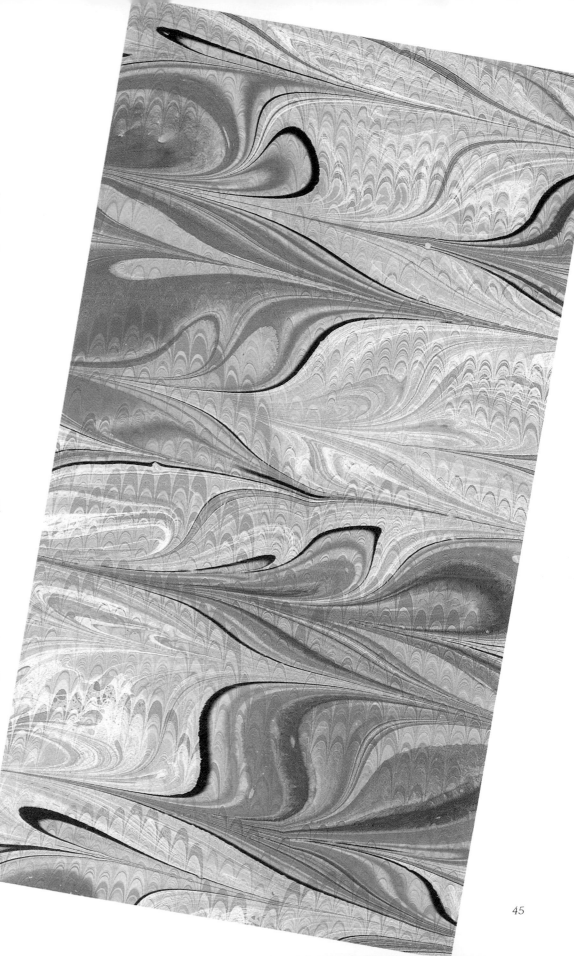

Applying Colors. Colors can be applied to the marbling size in a variety of ways to produce different effects. The type of tool used to drop the color, the amount of color applied, and whether color is uniformly distributed or concentrated in one section of the tray will all influence the appearance of the marbled image. In many traditional patterns, uniformity of design and color is important. Experiment with some of the specific patterns discussed beginning on page 50, but don't concentrate on producing them exclusively. Marbling is a creative medium, and impulsive or improvisational color delivery and combing can yield unique and expressive designs.

Using an Eyedropper. The impulse of most people using an eyedropper is to squeeze the rubber bulb to deposit a drop of liquid, and then to release the pressure, drawing in air before squeezing again. This technique will not work for marbling because air released with a drop of color will cause bubbles to form on the size. To use a dropper as a color applicator, fill it with well-stirred color, hold it close to the surface of the size, and squeeze the dropper very slightly, releasing just one drop of color. Maintain pressure on the bulb while moving the dropper to the next position. Then, applying a bit more pressure, release another single drop of color, as shown (below), alternating colors if you wish. Continue carefully to avoid releasing too much color.

Using a Dropper Bottle. The dropper bottle is used in the same way as the eyedropper. Squeeze gently and let the color drop from about 1″ (2.5 cm) or less above the size. Avoid squirting color, and shake the bottle gently from side to side periodically to move the stirring beads.

Using an Atomizer. Although somewhat difficult to master, an artist's atomizer is a useful tool for creating borders and bands of color on the marbling size. It can also be used to mist the entire size surface with color.

Different types of color applicators can be used to deliver varying sized drops of color.

Using a Whisk. Insert the whisk into a stirred and adjusted color, stir again, and tap the whisk on the edge of the color container to remove any excess paint or ink. Then, holding the whisk with one hand and keeping it about one foot above the tray, tap the wrapped end of the whisk against a stick, or against the forefinger of the other hand as shown (left), while simultaneously moving your hands over the size. Replenish color when necessary and continue applying it until the entire surface of the size has been sprinkled. If you want a more intense color, repeat the process. Color blends can be created by using an eyedropper to apply several colors onto the straws of the whisk as well. Gall water can be similarly applied to dilute colors and to create variegated color blends.

Droplet sizes will vary depending upon the amount of color in the whisk, the height at which the whisk is held, and the amount of vigor you use in tapping it. Be careful not to get too aggressive, as colors may begin to sink, or troublesome bubbles may appear on the size. Try to work as quickly and efficiently as possible; this will help minimize dust contamination of the size.

Using a Brush. A gentle approach is the best. A simple wrist-snap should release the paint from a loaded brush as shown (left). Too vigorous an approach may cause bubbles to form on the size.

Pattern-Making Concepts. Part of the fascination of marbling is that, although you can approach the craft as an experimental medium, you can also exercise considerable control over it if you have a knowledge of basic patterning techniques. Once you understand how shapes and patterns evolve, you can devise or simulate specific designs and decipher previously printed papers. The illustrations beginning on page 50 depict the consistently predictable results achieved by simple, methodical patterning. Practice some of the simple raking and combing movements shown here, and make some prints to familiarize yourself with equipment and procedures.

A smooth, continuous rake or comb movement will help keep your marbled patterns crisp and precise. Hold your tools in a way that allows you to make fluid, graceful passes through the colors.

Making the Print. Correctly laying a sheet of paper on the size requires some practice. Eventually you'll be able to apply the paper so that one edge of it makes immediate contact with the color and the remainder of the paper rolls smoothly onto the marbled pattern without shifting or flopping and trapping air. Your first marbled sheets, however, will probably show streaked areas, indicating paper movement, or unmarbled spots where an air bubble prevented image contact.

If your papers have been alumed correctly and kept flat, you won't have to contend with the added problem of trying to control paper that is buckled or wrinkled. Maintaining a high degree of humidity in the marbling room, and misting the alumed paper blotter periodically, will help keep the papers supple and cooperative.

The choreography involved in moving a sheet of paper from the alum stack to the marbling tray is as follows: 1) Lift the alum stack cover, pull one sheet of paper out by the nearest corner, and replace the cover on the stack. 2) Holding the sheet *alum-side-down* by two diagonal corners, bring your hands close enough together to slightly bow the paper and prevent the free corners from drooping. 3) Carry the paper to the tray with a minimum of movement so as to prevent it from becoming stiff or wrinkled. 4) Steady one hand on the far corner of the tray and, continuing to hold the paper, ease the far edge of it onto the size as shown (top left). 5) Smoothly lay the rest of the sheet onto the color pattern in one motion. 6) Once the sheet is down, hold it steady by the edge closest to you, and letting go of the far corner of the paper, tap against any ridges in the sheet. A hollow sound indicates an air bubble between the paper and color. Tapping it out will often allow you to avoid holes in simple patterns. 7) Let go of the near corner of the sheet when you're satisfied that it's made complete contact with the color. Once a print is made, it won't be disturbed by movement, and can easily be pulled back onto your rinse board as shown (middle and bottom).

To make a successful print, it is important to handle the paper in a relaxed manner. Left-handed marblers will find the hand position shown here most comfortable. Right-handed marblers will feel more steady if their right hand lowers the paper and their left holds it in place. As soon as a print is made the paper can be lifted out of the tray and laid directly on to the rinse board.

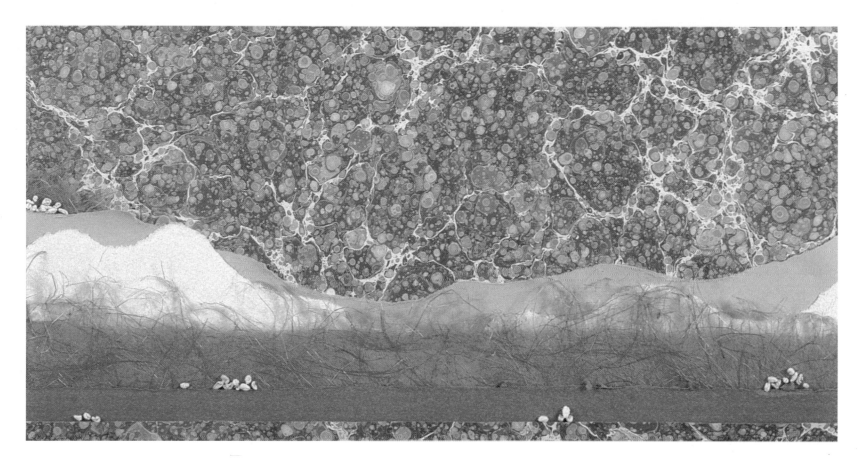

Rinsing and Drying. If you are working with a specially designed marbling tray, position your rinse board in the drain section and place a rinse bucket under the drain hole. If you're not using a special tray, hold your rinse board over a bucket or sink. Splash a few drops of water on the board to prevent the paper from sliding. Rinse as discussed earlier, on page 30. Avoid touching the print during the rinsing process; watercolor marbled papers are easily smeared while wet.

Dry and press the papers as discussed on page 30.

Fixing Marbled Papers. Some papers made with water-based paints will smudge or chalk slightly and should be fixed before they're used for projects. Coating them lightly with an acrylic spray, such as the kind used for fixing pastel drawings, will prevent any color from rubbing off when the papers are handled.

Cleanup. Because the materials used in watercolor marbling are water soluble, detergents won't be needed for cleaning equipment. Any soap residue can affect future marbling, so use water and a scrub brush instead of detergent.

Clean whisks by holding them under running water and flaring the straw until color is no longer released. Remove the caps from droppers and rinse both parts, using a pipe cleaner to remove any stubborn color. Rinse and wipe any size and color residue from brushes, combs, and rakes, and use water and a scrub brush on the remainder of your equipment. If you clean everything thoroughly, and cover your equipment during storage, you'll minimize dust and pollution problems in your next marbling session.

One in a series of stone-marbled landscapes, this collage is entitled "Red River Valley", and is composed of papers watercolor-marbled on a carrageenan size and other torn or rolled papers. The original is 16 × 29 inches (40 × 72 cm).

Traditional Patterns

There are a number of traditional marbled patterns that are based on specific combing techniques and color variations. Similar patterns sometimes have different names, and some marblers apply pattern names more loosely than others. There are those who would argue that the Nonpareil pattern is not authentic unless the comb used to create it has a particular-size tooth, and unless historic directions for making, applying, and combing the color are followed precisely. The patterns described here, although based on historic models, make no claim to being exact replicas of centuries-old designs.

To make the following patterns, complete the preliminary steps indicated (each letter corresponds to an illustration at the bottom of the page) as well as the final step in the small box near the design. Each illustration shows the direction to move combs and rakes and whether to use a straight or waved movement. If you use a comb or rake in the size indicated your pattern will look like the one pictured, but you can also experiment with other equipment sizes.

There are many more patterns possible than could be shown here. As you practice these designs you will see that most patterns are made by modifying others and perhaps discover a few of your own.

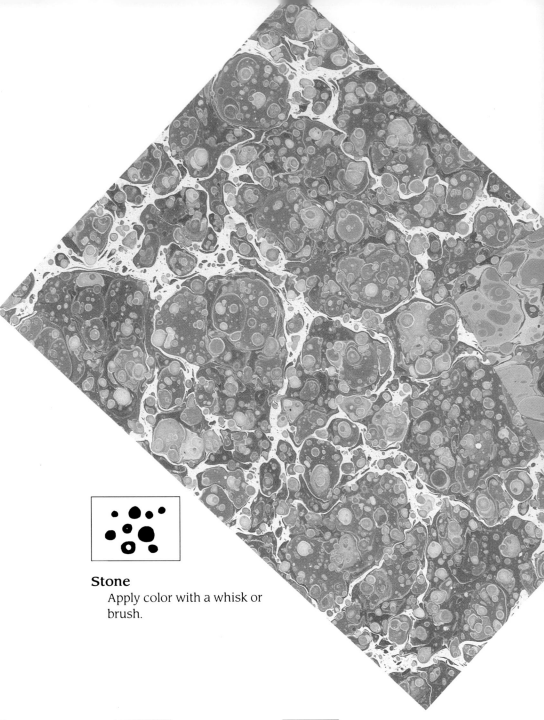

Stone
Apply color with a whisk or brush.

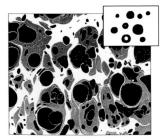

A Randomly apply color.

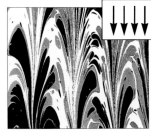

B Pull rake toward you.

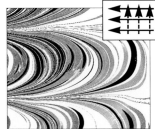

C Push away bisecting the previous pass.

D Rake right to left across the grain.

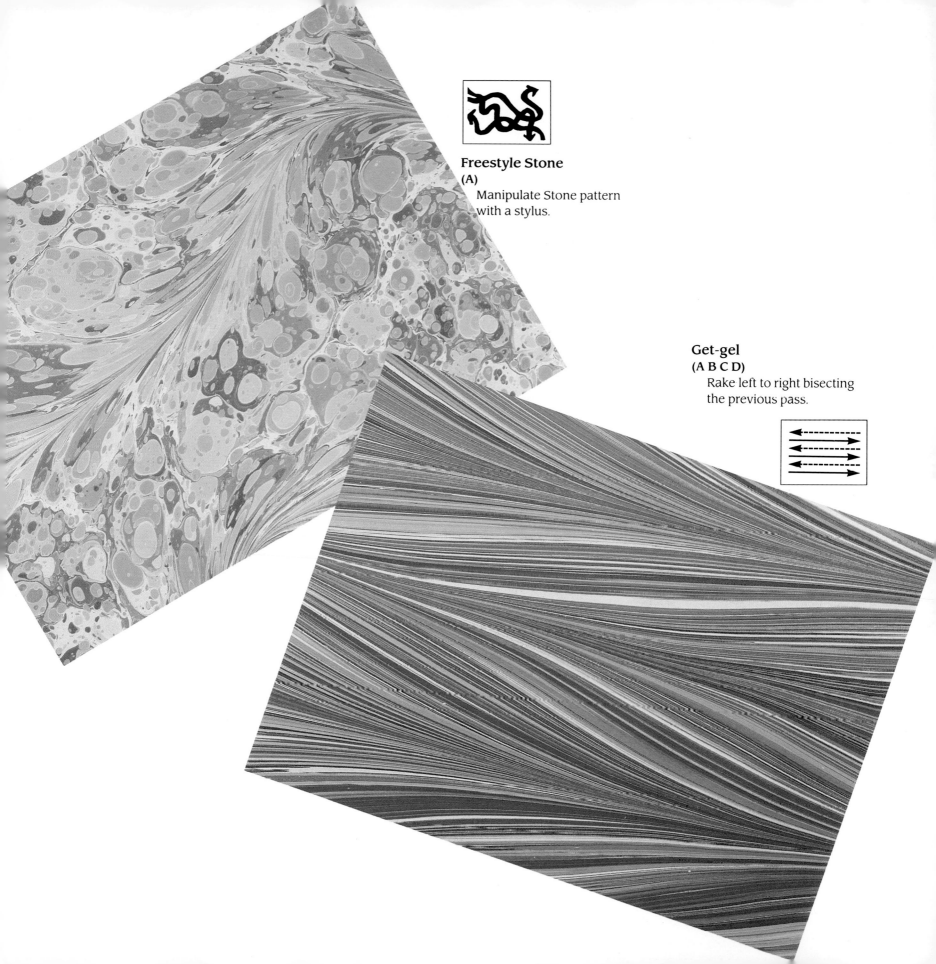

Freestyle Stone
(A)
Manipulate Stone pattern
with a stylus.

Get-gel
(A B C D)
Rake left to right bisecting
the previous pass.

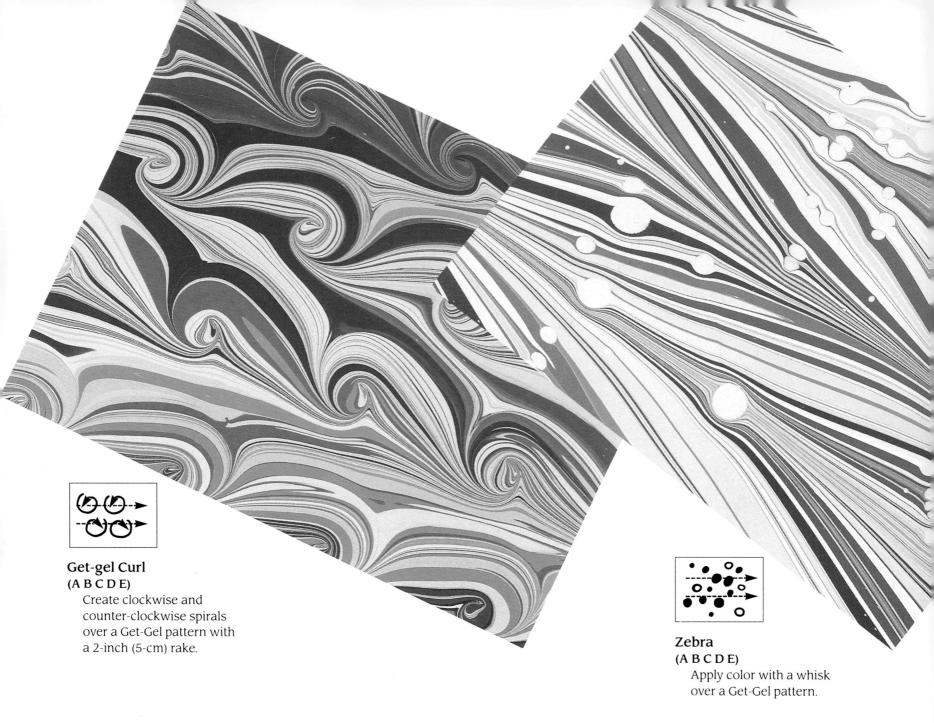

Get-gel Curl
(A B C D E)
Create clockwise and
counter-clockwise spirals
over a Get-Gel pattern with
a 2-inch (5-cm) rake.

Zebra
(A B C D E)
Apply color with a whisk
over a Get-Gel pattern.

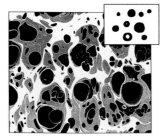

A Randomly apply color.

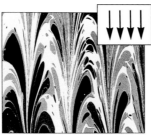

B Pull rake toward you.

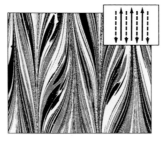

C Push away bisecting the
previous pass.

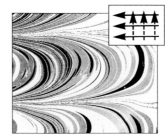

D Rake right to left across
the grain.

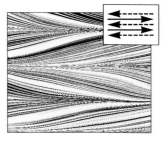

E Rake left to right bisecting
the previous pass.

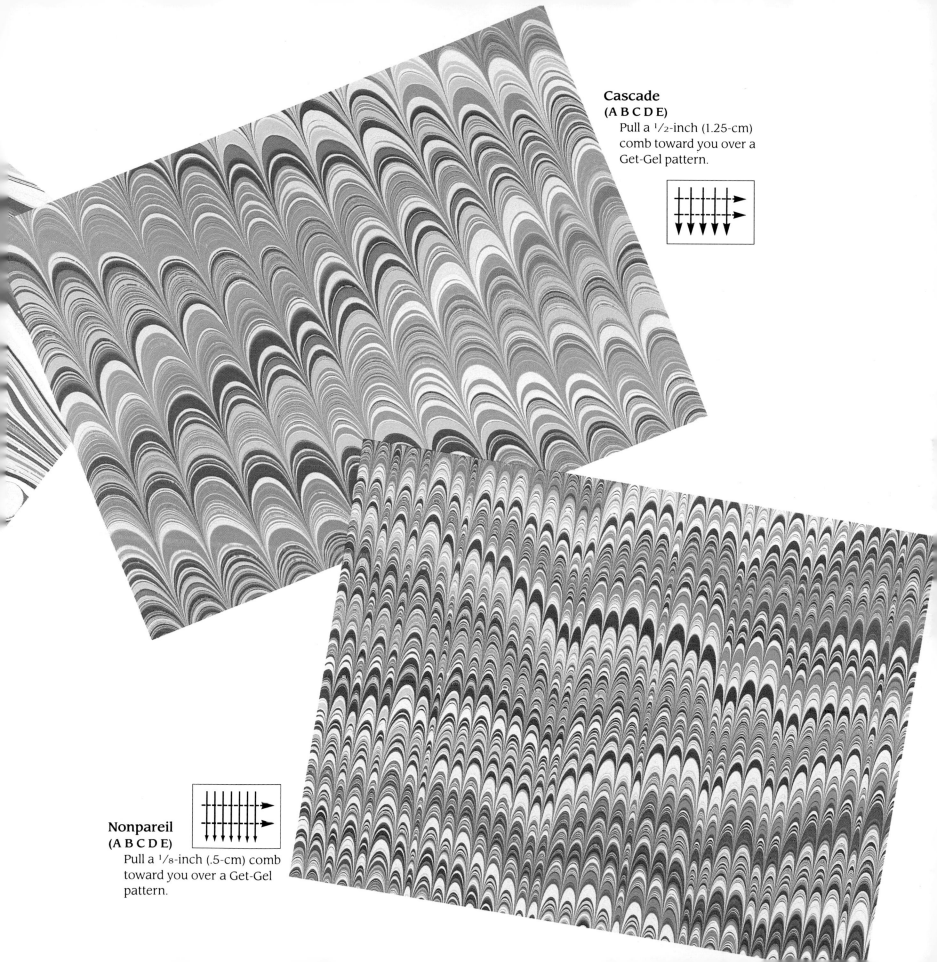

Cascade
(A B C D E)
Pull a 1/2-inch (1.25-cm) comb toward you over a Get-Gel pattern.

Nonpareil
(A B C D E)
Pull a 1/8-inch (.5-cm) comb toward you over a Get-Gel pattern.

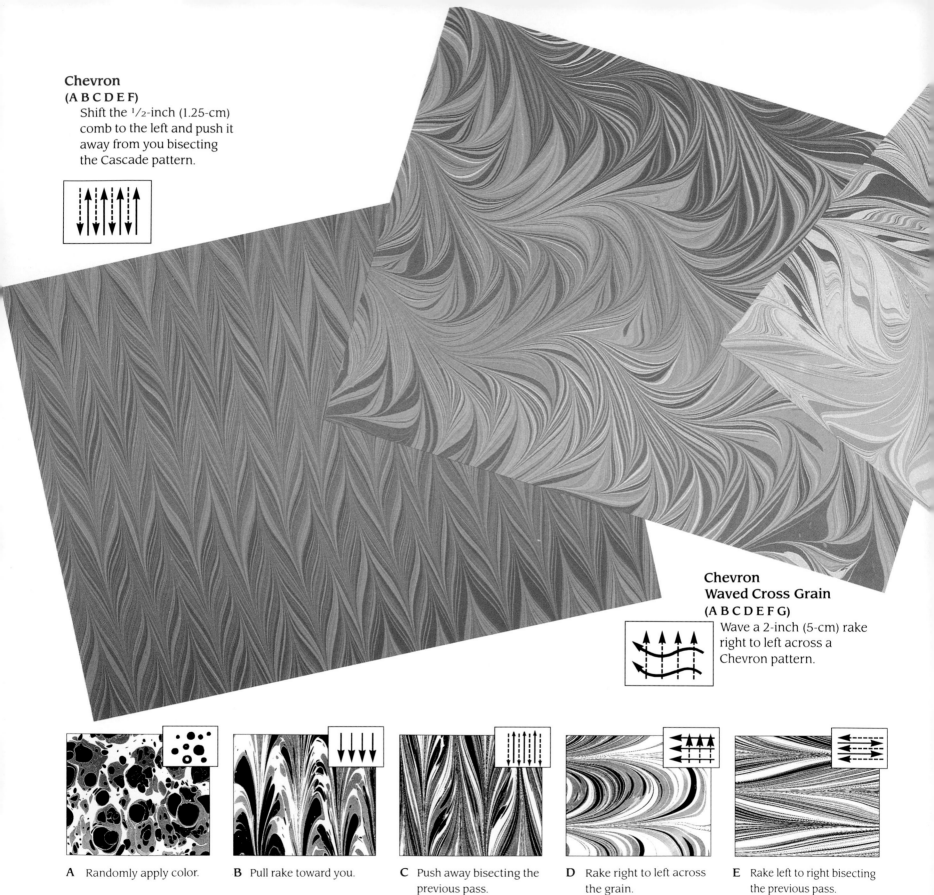

Chevron
(A B C D E F)

Shift the ¹/₂-inch (1.25-cm) comb to the left and push it away from you bisecting the Cascade pattern.

Chevron
Waved Cross Grain
(A B C D E F G)

Wave a 2-inch (5-cm) rake right to left across a Chevron pattern.

A Randomly apply color.

B Pull rake toward you.

C Push away bisecting the previous pass.

D Rake right to left across the grain.

E Rake left to right bisecting the previous pass.

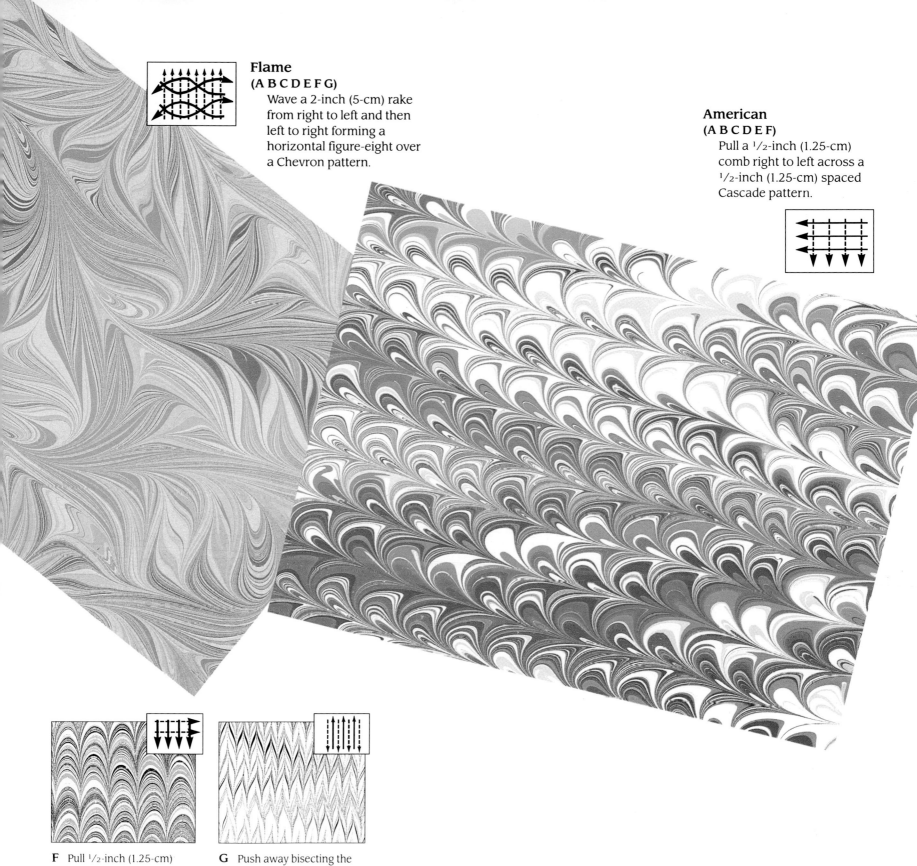

Flame
(A B C D E F G)
Wave a 2-inch (5-cm) rake
from right to left and then
left to right forming a
horizontal figure-eight over
a Chevron pattern.

American
(A B C D E F)
Pull a $\frac{1}{2}$-inch (1.25-cm)
comb right to left across a
$\frac{1}{2}$-inch (1.25-cm) spaced
Cascade pattern.

F Pull $\frac{1}{2}$-inch (1.25-cm)
comb toward you.

G Push away bisecting the
previous pass.

French Curl
(A B C D E H)

Create clockwise and counter-clockwise spirals over a Nonpareil pattern with a 3-inch (7.5-cm) rake.

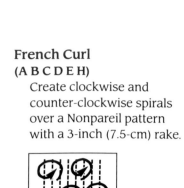

Waved Nonpareil
(A B C D E H)

Wave a 3-inch (7.5-cm) rake right to left across a Nonpareil pattern.

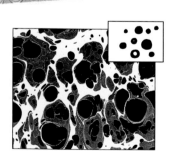

A Randomly apply color.

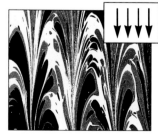

B Pull rake toward you.

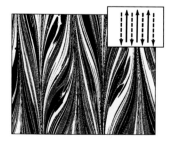

C Push away bisecting the previous pass.

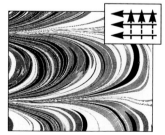

D Rake right to left across the grain.

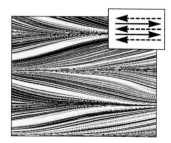

E Rake left to right bisecting the previous pass.

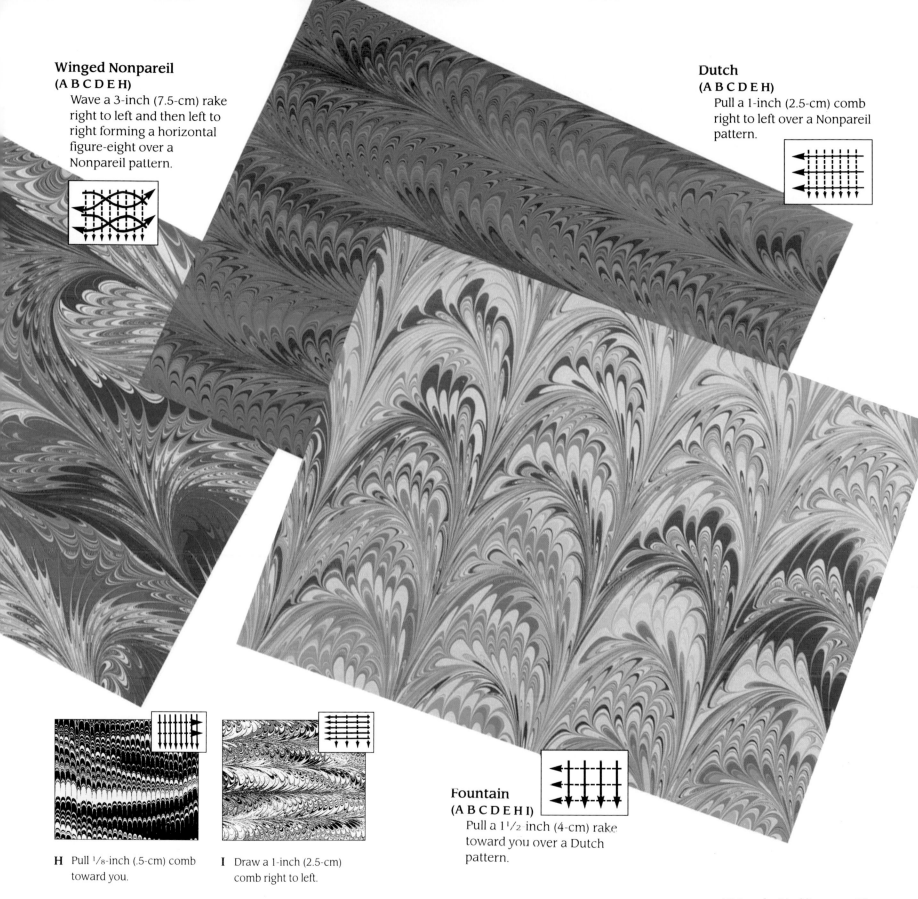

Winged Nonpareil
(A B C D E H)

Wave a 3-inch (7.5-cm) rake right to left and then left to right forming a horizontal figure-eight over a Nonpareil pattern.

Dutch
(A B C D E H)

Pull a 1-inch (2.5-cm) comb right to left over a Nonpareil pattern.

H Pull ⅛-inch (.5-cm) comb toward you.

I Draw a 1-inch (2.5-cm) comb right to left.

Fountain
(A B C D E H I)

Pull a 1½-inch (4-cm) rake toward you over a Dutch pattern.

Feather
(A B C D E H)

Draw a 1-inch (2.5-cm) comb right to left and then left to right across a Nonpareil pattern, waving the comb slightly on the return pass.

Bouquet
(A B C D E H)

Pull a Bouquet comb toward you in a squared off "S" movement over a Nonpareil pattern.

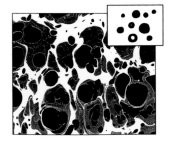

A Randomly apply color.

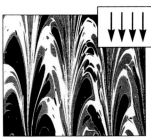

B Pull rake toward you.

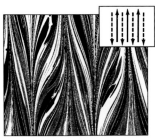

C Push away bisecting the previous pass.

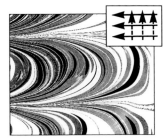

D Rake right to left across the grain.

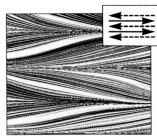

E Rake left to right bisecting the previous pass.

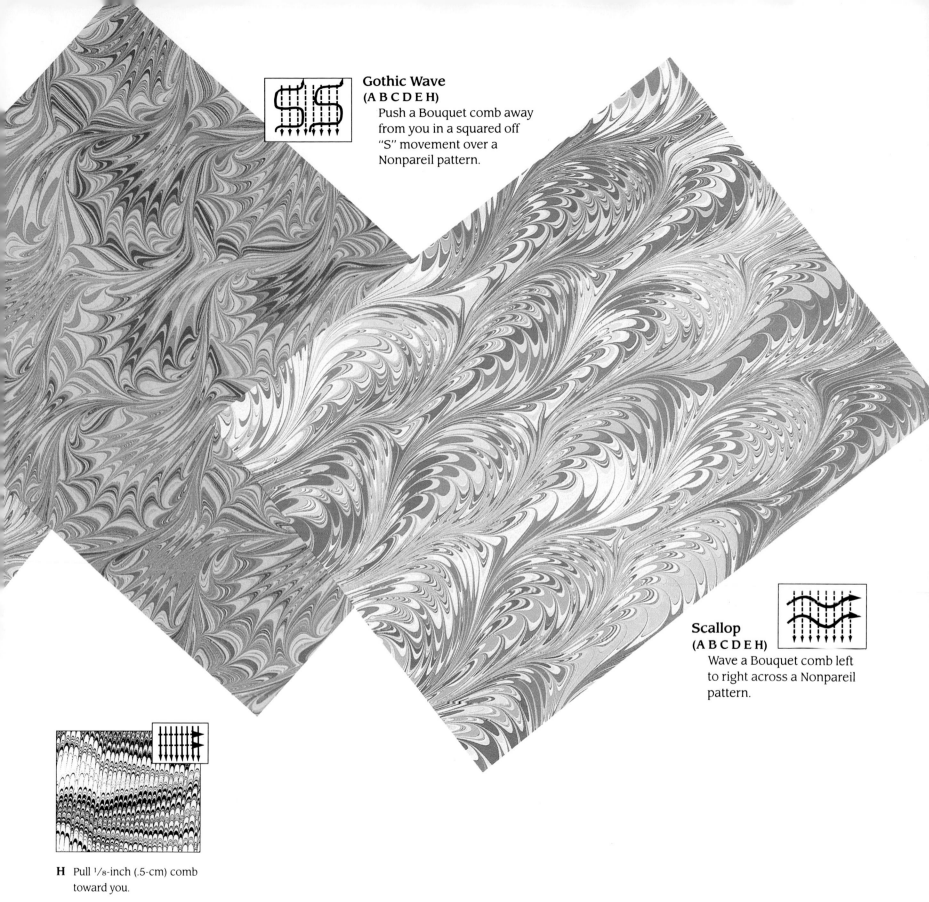

Gothic Wave
(A B C D E H)
Push a Bouquet comb away
from you in a squared off
"S" movement over a
Nonpareil pattern.

Scallop
(A B C D E H)
Wave a Bouquet comb left
to right across a Nonpareil
pattern.

H Pull ¹/₈-inch (.5-cm) comb
toward you.

Fantasy Patterns

Fantasy patterns are based on the plant and animal motifs seen in Persian marbling. Follow these step-by-step illustrations to create simple silhouetted flowers, birds, and fish in your marbled images. You can also create an overall fantasy image, such as a landscape or an abstract form, by marbling borders and bands of color and pattern.

Each shape begins from a round color droplet. The solid arrows in the illustrations indicate where to penetrate the color droplet with a stylus and which direction to move in. Note that sometimes the stylus is drawn through the droplet, while at other times (as in the beginning of the bird wing) it enters the design only partially. The broken arrows show the previous step.

To tease a color droplet into a flower, first draw a stylus (or a needle, toothpick, or piece of whisk straw) into the center of the color droplet. It will compress and separate the droplet where it enters. Petals are formed by then pulling the stylus away from the center of the droplet.

Troubleshooting

This chart illustrates problems sometimes experienced in watercolor marbling. Likely causes of the problems are listed in descending order of probability.

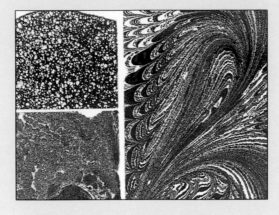

Color Sinks.

- Color lacks gall.
- Color is too thick.
- Size is too thick.
- Color was too aggressively applied.

Color Is Grainy.

- Color was inadequately mixed.
- Color was improperly stored.
- Color is sour or faulty.
- Color is contaminated with dust or mildew.

Image Appears Fuzzy.

- Size is too thick.
- Color is too thick.
- Too much time elapsed between color application and printing.
- Size is immature.

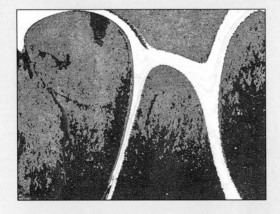

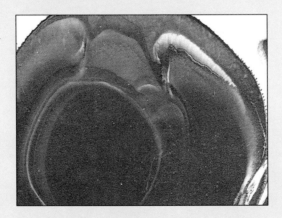

Color Does Not Adhere Well.

- Color was not well mixed.
- Color is too cold.
- Size is too cold.
- Size is too old.
- Alum is weak.
- Paper surface repelled the alum coating.
- Chemicals are present in the water.

Color Appears Mottled.

- Pigment was not properly mixed.
- Gall was not properly mixed.
- Color is contaminated.

Color Expands and Then Contracts.

- Size and color temperatures are too different.
- Color is too thick.
- Color was too heavily applied.

Image Appears Mushy.

- Pattern was overcombed.
- Size is old.
- Size is polluted.

Small Specks and Voids Appear on Pattern.

- Dust or other airborne matter has fallen on the size, colors, or paper.
- Alum has crystallized.

Image Has Serrated Edges, Small Ragged Voids, or Stars.

- Skin has formed on the size.
- Air is too dry.
- Too many chemicals are present in the water used in the size or in the colors.

Image Contains Blank Streaks, Blotches, or Areas with Faint Patterns.

- Aluming was done improperly.
- Paper was printed while still wet.

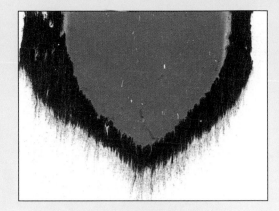

Color Streaks When Paper Is Rinsed.

- Color is too thick.
- Color was too heavily applied.
- Alum is too weak.

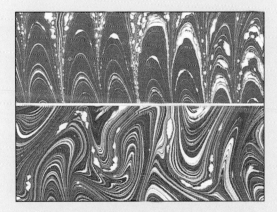

Globular Voids Appear in Image.

- Color contains too much gall.
- Excess gall has transferred to the size.
- Color and gall are not mixed together.

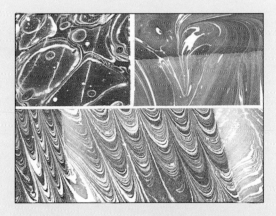

Light or Dark Lines Appear in Pattern.

- Paper was moved during printing.

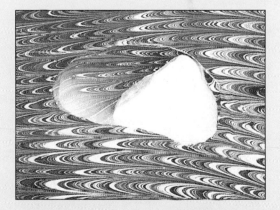

Large Void Appears in Pattern.

- An air bubble was trapped under the paper during printing.

Chapter Five
Oil-Color Marbling

OIL-COLOR MARBLING, PROBABLY THE LEAST EXPLORED OF THE MARBLING mediums, is much more tolerant than its watercolor relative. In oil-color marbling, dry air is not as critical a problem, dust has little adverse effect, and the temperature of the marbling room is not as important. Papers don't need to be treated, as oil colors readily stick to most surfaces and usually float and spread without difficulty. There is a trade-off, however: Images achieved in oil-color marbling are not as precise or as controllable as watercolor images, the cleanup process is more involved, and fumes from the paint and thinner are part of the experience. Still, oil patterns can be appreciated for the fact that they *lack* a controlled appearance. Oil-color images have a painterly quality, a richness and substance much like the colors used to make the images.

Multiple-image oil marbling made in three layers.

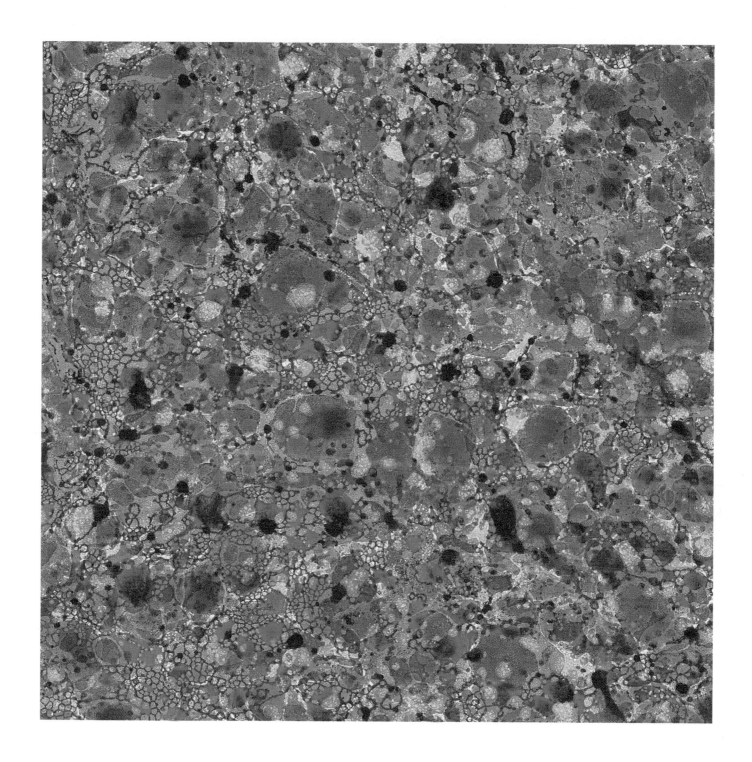

Southwest Memory

Equipment

Most of the equipment used in oil-color marbling is also used in watercolor marbling, and you may be tempted to use the same tray and tools. It would be wise to build separate trays and combing implements, however, if you plan to return to the watercolor method. Any trace of oil paint or thinner can cause mayhem if introduced into your watercolor size.

In addition to the equipment detailed beginning on page 22, you will also need the following:

- A pot, for making the optional methyl cellulose size
- A mask, to protect you from paint and thinner fumes
- Color containers made of glass or metal
- Stirring sticks, and possibly a mortar and pestle, for mixing oil paints.

The Workspace

Oil color marbling is usually not affected by the workspace environment. Some humidity will help keep the papers supple and make them easier to handle, but a vaporizer won't be needed, as it is in watercolor marbling. However, be sure to provide some kind of ventilation—an exhaust fan or an open window, for example. This may cause some dust to blow into the tray, but it won't seriously affect oil-color patterns. Caution should be used when handling and storing oil paints and thinners, as most are potentially harmful to humans and animals.

Materials

The Size. Powdered carrageenan or methyl cellulose is generally used for making the size. Oil marbling is sometimes done on water alone, although paints wander on an unthickened size and can't be patterned.

Water. Plain tap water, regardless of impurities, can be used for oil marbling.

Colors. Oil colors come in paste and in liquid form. Paste colors include artist's printing inks used for lithography and etching, artist's oils, and textile and serigraph inks. Commercial printing inks used for offset and letterpress give especially fine results. Liquid colors include Dryad Linmarblin colors, sign-painting enamels, enamel house-paints, and automotive lacquers. The gold and silver enamel paints commonly sold in hardware stores usually work well, although sometimes you have to strain out troublesome lumps.

Oils. Linseed oil is used to soften paste colors.

Dispersing Agents. Photo Flo™ or common dish detergent can be used to help problem colors spread.

Paint Thinner. Mineral spirits serve three functions in oil marbling: to dilute color, to disperse color, and to clean equipment.

Cleansers. Powdered cleansers may be used to clean the marbling tray, while hand soap is needed for a final cleaning of brushes and whisks after they have been cleaned in mineral spirits.

Papers. Most papers can be oil marbled. The only ones to avoid are those that break down when wet, or those that are so highly polished or coated that they repel the paint.

Shifting the paper as the print was made helped create the mountain-like structures in this monoprint entitled "Southwest Memory" by Paul Maurer. This piece was made with oil marbling on a carrageenan size and pastel drawing. The original is 23 × 29 inches (58 × 72 cm).

Making the size. Instructions for making a methyl cellulose size and a carrageenan size appear on pages 31 and 41. Either type can be used for oil-color marbling. Methyl cellulose is a bit less expensive, and since crisp, well-defined images are not part of oil marbling, it will work quite well. The fact that methyl cellulose doesn't break down as quickly as carrageenan is another reason to use the former. Either type of size may be used immediately; when oil marbling, you needn't wait for the carrageenan to age.

Skimming the Size. Skim as for watercolor marbling to clean the size between prints. (See page 42.)

Preparing Colors. Oil colors are softened with linseed oil and diluted with mineral spirits before use. Even liquid oils benefit from the addition of a bit of linseed oil; colors tend to remain brighter if linseed oil is added before they're diluted. However, it's important to be diligent about mixing the paint, oil, and thinner together completely. If the materials are not homogenized, the marbling color will bead excessively, disperse irregularly, or contain lumps, making it difficult to pattern.

Mixing Liquid Oil-Color. To thin and mix liquid oils, pour a 1″ (2.5-cm) depth of well-stirred color into a container and, while stirring, add linseed oil (no more than twenty percent of the amount of paint) and enough thinner to bring the color to a milky consistency.

Mixing Paste Oil-Color. Start with about 2 tablespoons (50 g) of paste color, and add some linseed oil (about one-quarter of the amount of paste). Using a large dowel or stick, push, smear, and stir the oil into the color until the paste becomes smooth. Add more linseed oil, enough to bring the color to a creamy consistency. If the color is gritty or stringy, you may have to mix it with a mortar and pestle. When the color is well creamed, stir in enough thinner to bring the mixture to a milky consistency.

Creating a Color Palette. To give yourself a good palette of colors for marbling, mix colors using the chart shown on page 44.

Adjusting and Testing Colors. Oil colors don't sink as readily as other coloring agents; they show their reluctance to cooperate by refusing to spread and forming tiny beads of color instead. Sometimes a particular color greatly alters the surface tension in the tray when it is added to the size. When the next color applied attempts to spread, it encounters a resistance it can't overcome. There are two ways to deal with this situation: You can apply the colors in various sequences until you determine which colors follow each other successfully; or you can add more thinner to problem colors to make them spread. A dispersing agent such as Photo-Flo™ can be used in place of thinner. In addition to helping the colors spread, a dispersant will also make them reticulate. Be sure not to dilute your colors so much that they lose their vividness, however.

Applying Colors. Apply oil colors as in watercolor marbling (see page 46), except that you needn't work quickly. Oil colors are constantly moving and patterning themselves; interesting images can be achieved simply by applying colors, walking away for an hour or so, and then returning to make the print.

Oil colors start patterning themselves as soon as they touch the size. You can take your time when marbling with oil paints; you might even walk away from your tray for an hour or so before making the print. These three prints were made by applying color to the size and then printing them at different times in separate sections of the same tray. The first print (left) was pulled one minute after the colors were applied. When 15 minutes had passed, a second print was made (middle). In 60 minutes, the oil colors arranged themselves into a lacey matrix of color (right).

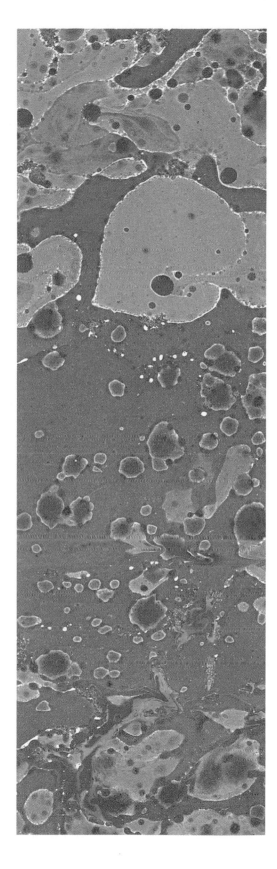 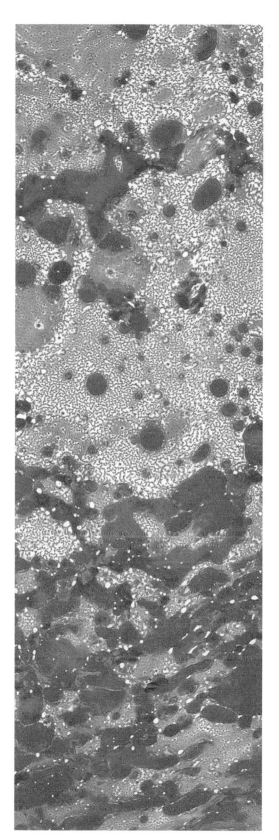 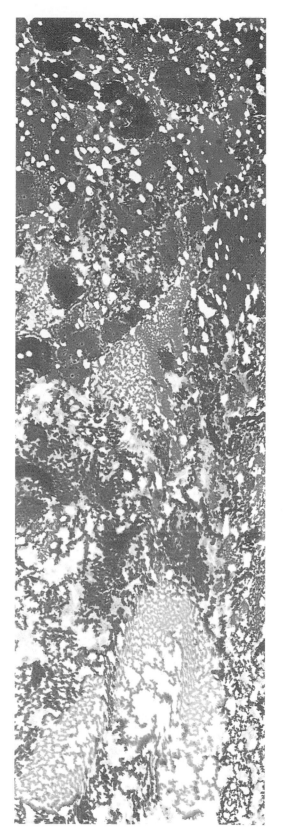

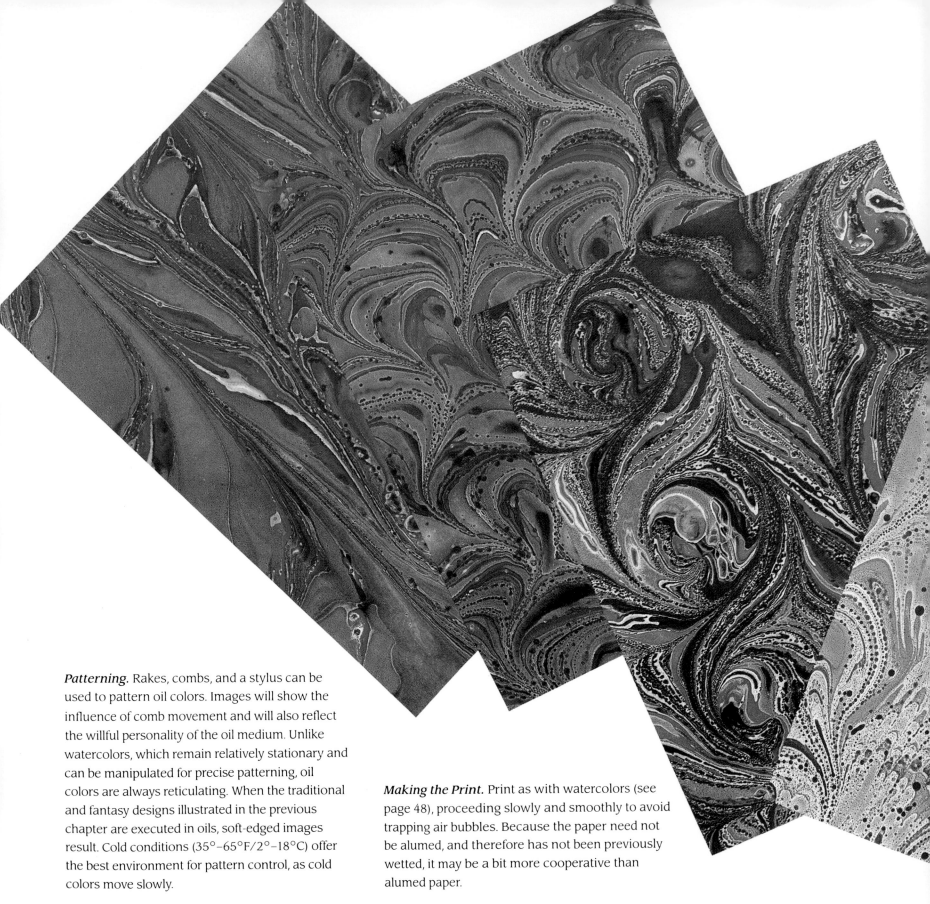

Patterning. Rakes, combs, and a stylus can be used to pattern oil colors. Images will show the influence of comb movement and will also reflect the willful personality of the oil medium. Unlike watercolors, which remain relatively stationary and can be manipulated for precise patterning, oil colors are always reticulating. When the traditional and fantasy designs illustrated in the previous chapter are executed in oils, soft-edged images result. Cold conditions (35°–65°F/2°–18°C) offer the best environment for pattern control, as cold colors move slowly.

Making the Print. Print as with watercolors (see page 48), proceeding slowly and smoothly to avoid trapping air bubbles. Because the paper need not be alumed, and therefore has not been previously wetted, it may be a bit more cooperative than alumed paper.

Rinsing and Drying. The rinsing process is the same as in watercolor marbling. Blot or pick off any excess pigment.

Oil-color papers take a long time to dry—days, in humid conditions. Although drying in damp conditions tends to render oil-color papers more wrinkle free, you may want to dry your papers in a warm or sunny room to speed up the process. Press them between sheets of absorbent paper to remove stubborn dampness.

Cleaning the Equipment. Wipe the tray and patterning tools with a dry paper towel to remove any moisture, and then rub the equipment with a cloth soaked in turpentine or mineral spirits to remove any oil-color residue. When the equipment appears clean, rinse it, and then scrub it with a brush and powdered cleanser to remove the solvent film. Finally, rinse the equipment very thoroughly.

Use thinner to clean brushes and whisks, allowing paint-hardened areas to soak until the paint has loosened. Rinse the brushes and whisks in warm water, and then work dish detergent or hand soap into them to remove the solvent film. Rinse the brushes and whisks well, and reshape them to dry. Clean eyedroppers with solvent and then with soap, using a pipe cleaner to reach all parts of the cap and dropper.

Patterning oil paints (left to right) with a stylus, comb, or rake produces a looser, more abstract image with its own charm. The Bouquet pattern is a stippled rendition of the watercolor Bouquet pattern on page 58.

Troubleshooting

Color Streaks When Rinse Water Is Applied.

If a color is too heavily applied, or if it is too thick, it may bleed as papers are rinsed. Large beads or lumps of color that run can be blotted with the twisted tip of a paper towel or with a cotton swab.

Color Is Grainy or Forms Small Lumps.

Some beading of color is part of the nature of oil marbling. If the color is excessively grainy or lumpy, however, it usually means that it has not been mixed thoroughly or that the color is old or dirty. To attempt to solve the problem, strain the color and remix it. If that doesn't work, it may be that something in the chemical makeup of the color renders it incompatible with the thinning agent.

Color Sinks When Applied.

This rarely happens in oil marbling. If a color does sink, it indicates that the color is not diluted enough, that the size or color is exceptionally cold, that you're being too aggressive in your color application, or that you haven't skimmed thoroughly enough.

Chapter Six
Fabric Marbling

FABRIC MARBLING, AN INCREASINGLY POPULAR FORM OF FABRIC DESIGN, HAS BEEN practiced for at least a century. The medium, once used to decorate book cloth, is now used to decorate wearing apparel from hats to shoes, and is used by fiber artists in tapestries and soft sculpture. New fabric paints are being discovered almost daily, and formulas are being devised to make the colors suitable for marbling. Oil paints, acrylics, fabric dyes and paints, sumi colors, and air-brush inks can all be used on different types of fabric. Watercolor marbling paints and inks can also be used for pieces that don't need to be washed, such as wall hangings. The smorgasbord of coloring agents available can be tried on any number of fabrics—natural or synthetic. Crêpe de Chine, Charmeuse and Habotai silks, as well as synthetic satins, cotton broadcloth, and cotton knits, will all marble successfully.

Satin oil-marbled with a stencil by Sandra Holzman. The fabric measures 36 × 45 inches (90 × 102 cm).

In general, I find silks and synthetic fabrics to be the most receptive to marbling. Coarse and loose weaves usually do not produce satisfactory results. Fabrics that contain fire retardants, dirt repellent finishes, permanent press finishes, or other miracle treatments will probably not be very cooperative, either.

Prewashing and Testing Fabrics

Always wash and thoroughly rinse the fabric to be marbled, in order to remove any sizing it may contain. It's a good idea to test a sample of any particular fabric before purchasing yards of it to marble. Samples of pre-washed, unadulterated fabrics available from textile-art suppliers such as Brooks & Flynn can help you in your fabric choice.

Handling the Fabric

If you've mastered the art of laying down paper for marbling without trapping pockets of air or unintentionally shifting the sheet (see page 48), you probably won't have too much difficulty handling fabric. The fluidity of the fabric compared to that of paper is not the problem one might expect. At least you won't have to worry about your material becoming stiff and uncooperative, like some overdried papers. For small pieces of fabric, or to single out small areas for decoration, you can use an embroidery hoop to hold the fabric taut. Sheets of cardboard can be inserted into pillowcases or other tubular materials, such as T-shirts, if you like to work with a semi-rigid surface. Having a marbling assistant is ideal for working with lengths of fabric, provided you synchronize your movements to your partner's. You can work solo by tacking the edges of your fabric to dowels or balsa-wood strips cut slightly shorter than the length of your tray. Holding one dowel in each hand will enable you to control a length of fabric as you lower it onto the size. Long pieces of bamboo with pins at either end, called "Shenshi," can be purchased and used to control fabric in the same way.

To marble fabric that's supported by embroidery hoops or cardboard inserts, slowly tip the fabric onto the size. For loose fabric that's attached to dowels or hand held, let the center of the cloth droop down to touch the surface of the size first. Then, slowly and smoothly, lower the ends onto the size. A controlled movement is necessary to prevent blank hesitation marks or air-bubble voids from ruining your design.

A wide range of fabrics can be marbled. The Bouquet-patterned silk scarf in this picture was made by Polly Fox with acrylic paints on a carrageenan size. The pillows by Paul are oil-marbled on a cotton/polyester blend. The watercolor wall piece is mine, entitled "Zephyr."

Fabric Marbling With Oil Paints

The oil paints used to marble fabric can be floated on a size of carrageenan or of methyl cellulose (see page 41 or 31). For very fluid designs, you may even want to try floating paints on plain water. Prepare the paints as though they were being used for paper marbling (see page 68). For small pieces of fabric, such as pillow covers or T-shirts, you may be able to use your oil marbling tray. For larger pieces of fabric, such as scarves or skirts, you can build a makeshift tray by stretching heavy plastic over a wooden frame.

Because you're using oil paints, the fabric needn't be mordanted. You should, however, wash, dry, and iron the fabric to remove any sizing or wrinkles.

Procedures

Apply your paints with brushes or whisks as with oil paints on paper, then pattern (see pages 68 to 70), or let the paints reticulate to form their own designs. Apply the fabric to the size, letting it rest for a moment to pick up the paints. Rinse by gently swirling the fabric in a tub of water, or by gently hosing off the fabric if you're working outside or near a utility sink. Gently squeeze out the water and hang the fabric to dry. The colors will need to cure for about two weeks before they are permanent. Most of the paint and thinner fumes will dissipate during this time. After the colors have set, hand wash the fabric, then iron it, placing it between pieces of cotton broadcloth.

Fabric Marbling With Acrylics

Acrylic paints, like oils, can be floated on a carrageenan or a methyl cellulose size (see page 41 or 31). You will have to alum the fabric and build or buy a separate tray for marbling with acrylics. You may also want to construct a separate set of combs and rakes. Although acrylic paint is technically a water-based medium, it quickly dries to a rubbery consistency. Using tools with any acrylic residue left on them causes spots and voids to appear in traditional watercolor marbling. To keep your tools in good shape, clean them in warm water as soon as possible after marbling.

Colors

Many brands of acrylic paint, such as Deka® and Liquitex® are available in tube or in liquid form. Some are especially prepared for marbling and may need no adulteration. Others may need to be thinned only slightly or diluted by as much as fifty percent with distilled water. In general, acrylic paints should be about the consistency of thin cream. Color intensities and the amount of dispersion will vary from brand to brand. Always test color before diluting it or adding a dispersant such as Photo-Flo.™ As with watercolors, a separate testing tray is helpful to avoid contaminating the size.

Most acrylics will float and spread without difficulty. If some colors sink when others are applied to the test tray, try using them in a different sequence. If you find you need to use a dispersant to keep some colors from sinking, use Photo-Flo™; it's more compatible than ox gall with acrylics.

If your colors seem gritty or mottled, it may be that the pigment is separating from the binder. Remix the colors until they're well homogenized. One marbler friend of mine uses a whisk attached to a power drill, with good results. Another trick to smoothing out colors and helping the pigment bind properly is to add acrylic varnish, up to about twenty-five percent of the volume of your color.

Preparing Fabrics.

Although some thicker fabrics may need to soak in an alum bath for up to half an hour, most will print well with acrylics if saturated with a solution of about 3 tablespoons (75 g) of alum to 1 quart (.9 liters) of water. Squeeze out the alum solution gently and hang the mordanted cloth to dry. Then, to remove all wrinkles, iron it at a setting appropriate to the fabric type. Any creases will distort the way the fabric picks up the colors and pattern.

Procedures.

Apply colors with brushes, whisks, droppers, or dropper bottles, and pattern as desired (see pages 46 to 61). Finely tuned acrylics should give you the same level of pattern definition as that achieved with watercolor paints. Most of the combing instructions offered in Chapter 4 can be used with acrylics. Since most acrylics tend to be somewhat translucent, however, you may need to apply more color to achieve strong color intensity.

Silk scarves in oil, acrylic, and suminagashi marbling. The knotted scarves with the delicate combed design are by Iris Nevins.

Cleaning the size is particularly important when working with acrylics; skim frequently to keep the size in good condition. Often, when acrylics begin to sink during a marbling session, a thorough subsurface skimming will solve the problem. Acrylics tend to dry out quickly when exposed to air, so you may find them gradually becoming too thick to use correctly. If this occurs, add enough distilled water to the paints to bring them back to working consistency.

Apply the fabric to the size with smooth, deliberate motions, as discussed on page 74. Let the fabric rest on the colors for about half a minute before removing it to a bucket of clean rinse-water. Gently squeeze water from the rinsed fabric and hang it to dry. Acrylic colors need to be heat-set by ironing the fabric on the wrong side with as hot an iron as the fabric can accept, or by placing the fabric in a hot dryer for about forty-five minutes. As with oil-marbled fabric, it's best to let the colors cure for a week or so, at which point you can hand wash the fabric in mild soap, dry it, and give it a final pressing.

Suminagashi Fabric Marbling

Boku Undo colors (see page 26) can be used on fabric as well as on paper. Silks take these colors especially well without any aluming. Neopaque fabric paints also lend themselves well to sumi fabric marbling, although it will be necessary to alum the fabric before marbling.

Procedures.

Wash, dry, alum (if necessary), and iron the fabric to be marbled. Apply colors (see page 28), then apply the fabric as discussed on page 74, and allow it to soak up the patterned colors. Rinse the marbled fabric in a bucket of clean water, and hang it to dry. Cure the color by allowing the fabric to hang for twenty-four hours, then iron to set the color, hand wash, and press.

Marbling With Other Coloring Agents

Fabric paints such as those made by Texicolor and Tulip, and airbrush inks such as those made by Probrite and Versatex, are sold through textile-art supply houses. Although they generally perform like acrylics, some need to be thinned or heat-set in a particular way. Most reputable suppliers will provide instructions for using their products that, along with the basic directions provided here, can guide you in further fabric marbling adventures.

Years ago when the rest of us were still novice marblers, Peggy Skycraft was marbling tents. This is "Sunrise", an 8 × 8 × 8 foot (240 cm) beauty created in 1978, made with acrylic marbling on nylon and embellished with beads and feathers.

Chapter Seven
Friskets, Experiments, and Marbling Objects

BY THE TIME YOU REACH THIS CHAPTER, YOU'VE PROBABLY SPENT A GREAT DEAL OF
energy perfecting several marbling techniques (or at least reading about them).
You know how to mix paints and sizes to the right consistency, how to
apply papers and fabrics with graceful assurance, and how to do precise
combing. Now it's time to relax a bit, begin breaking the
rules you've learned, and really have fun. If you've mastered the art
of applying your paper so that it makes complete contact with the color and
doesn't sport "holes" in the pattern, it's time to learn how to *prevent* the
paper from taking the color evenly. Several renegade techniques are
discussed later in the chapter. For now, try a more respectable
method of altering a marbled image: the frisket.

This overmarbled print, a simple Get-gel over a waved
Nonpareil, was enhanced by shifting the paper.

Friskets

A frisket is a device used to preserve an unmarbled area within a marbled pattern. Sometimes a frisket creates a clear space for drawing or lettering on a print, but often the unmarbled silhouette serves as decoration. There are several kinds of friskets; some are easy to make and use, while others require some dexterity with a swivel knife. Depending upon what kind of image you want to preserve, you may decide to block out a shape or some lettering with liquid frisket, to cut a simple paper mask, or to create an intricate cutout with frisket film. Although drawing and lettering abilities are helpful, they are not essential; designs can be traced from magazine or book illustrations and transferred to frisket sheets by using carbon paper.

Simple Friskets

Just how simple a frisket can be is illustrated on the next page. The print shown was made by accident one night when a moth flew under a paper that was being marbled. Lifted out of the tray on a feather, the "frisket" flew off—slightly marbled, but seemingly unimpressed by the experience. We're not recommending that you marble living things. Try floating a paper cutout, a pressed flower, or a leaf on the patterned colors.

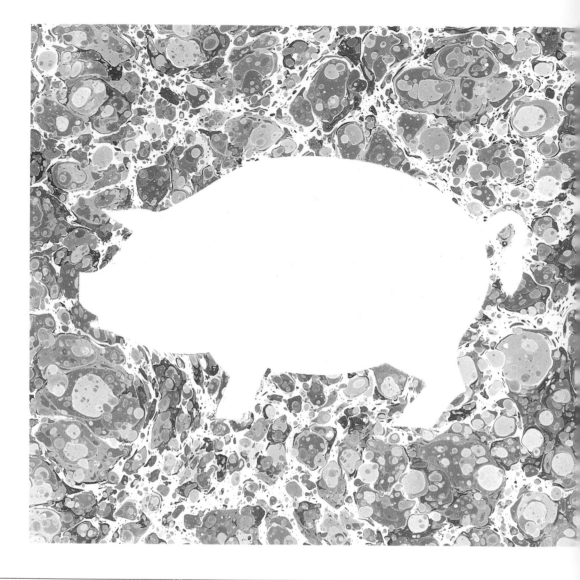

Piggyback Friskets

The piggyback technique involves taping a frisket to a sheet of paper and marbling both materials at the same time. The unmarbled silhouette produced when a paper cutout is carried piggyback into the marbling tray is shown on this page. The paper from which the pig was removed can also be used as a frisket. When taped to a sheet of paper and marbled, it produces the image of a pig.

To make a piggyback frisket, you'll need a pencil, some drafting tape or surgeon's tape, a sheet of medium-weight acetate or clear adhesive shelf-paper, a cutting mat or a sheet of glass, and a sharp swivel knife or an X-Acto® knife. Scissors,

although less efficient, can be used for cutting friskets, but you'll have to tape any extra slits made by the scissors if you want to use the paper from which the cutout is removed as a frisket, too.

A simple frisket can be made by outlining a shape on a piece of matte acetate and cutting the shape out. If you'd prefer to silhouette a magazine illustration, you should waterproof the illustration by covering both sides of the magazine page with clear adhesive shelf paper, and then cut out your silhouette frisket. Keeping silhouette shapes simple will allow you the best chance of a clean final image.

The piggyback frisket is highlighted by a dense marbled background. An airy design wouldn't silhouette the pig as well.

Although friskets can be applied to most papers with tape, soft printmaking papers and oriental papers will often be marred when the tape is removed after marbling. Test papers before applying friskets to see whether tape removal will harm them.

Apply the frisket by making small rings of tape, sticky side out, placing them on the back of the cutout, and pressing the cutout in place on the sheet to be marbled. Flatten the frisket as much as possible, paying special attention to its edges, where color could seep under during marbling. When you're sure the edges are down, make the print. (If you're marbling with watercolors, alum the paper and attached frisket before printing.)

Remove the frisket while rinsing, and use a soft brush to coax off any watercolor that has seeped under the mask. Oil color can't be removed, so be especially diligent about applying friskets when using oils. Clean and dry the frisket before using it to make another print.

Frisket Film

Frisket film (available at art supply stores) is used for making cutouts that would be difficult to tape down piggyback style. Because it's applied and burnished, or rubbed, onto the sheet to be marbled, there's less chance of seepage ruining the masked design. Frisket film can be difficult to apply, however, and each mask can be used only once.

To begin the frisket, outline a form directly on the frisket film, or transfer a silhouette from a book or magazine onto the film by tracing over carbon paper. Test the paper to be marbled to determine if film can be applied and removed without damaging the sheet. Then cut out the frisket, peel the film from its backing paper, and smooth the cutout onto the paper to be marbled. Burnish the frisket lightly, and proceed with marbling (or with aluming and marbling if you're using watercolors). After printing, rinse the marbled paper thoroughly, and while it's still wet, carefully peel the film off the print.

Liquid Frisket

Using liquid frisket, you can paint or letter directly on the paper to be marbled. The brush or pen strokes will be faithfully reproduced when the mask is removed. Liquid frisket can be used full strength, or diluted and then dripped or splattered on papers to create abstract designs. Papers to be watercolor marbled should be alumed before applying the frisket, as the mordanting process could disturb the liquid-frisket designs.

To mask papers with liquid frisket, apply the material with a pen or a brush. Allow the liquid to dry before marbling the sheet. Rinse the print as usual after marbling, and when it is thoroughly dry, gently peel the frisket off.

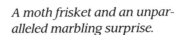

A moth frisket and an unparalleled marbling surprise.

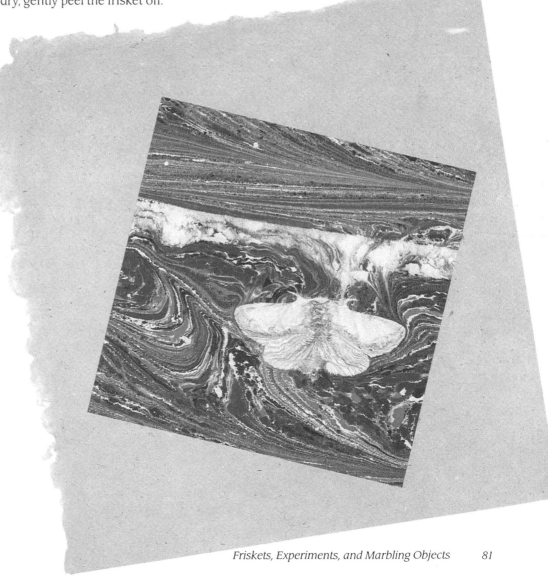

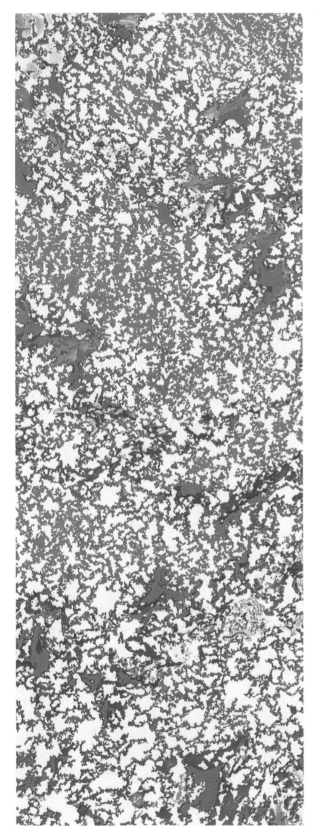

Experiments

All manner of suspicious behavior has passed under the guise of "performing marbling experiments." Perhaps those bizarre elixirs of catsup, cola, and salt some of us mixed in our youth still linger deliciously in our minds. I've seen the look of a mad scientist cross a marbler's face when encouraged to experiment by adding cosmetics to marbling colors. Encouraged to marble three-dimensional objects, students in one class, caught shorthanded, volunteered their lunches. Bananas and apples soon took on lively hues along with picture frames, sea shells, and make-up cases.

It may seem odd to those around you when you begin rummaging through the medicine cabinet and the pantry in search of color additives, and it may seem stranger still when you distort a beautiful combed pattern by rocking the marbling tray; but that's how new techniques are discovered. Experiments won't always be successful, but the pleasant surprises will usually outweigh the failures.

The following experiments often pollute the size. It's a good idea to attempt them after traditional marbling patterns are completed, or to make new size to continue more controllable work.

Color Additives

There is historical precedent for adding all manner of ingredients to colors in order to explore the effects in the marbling tray. Early European marblers added various oils and spirits to their colors to cause them to become grainy or mottled, and to push them into a network of fine veins. Modern-day oils found in cosmetics, pharmaceuticals, and cleaning products, as well as food oils like olive oil and peanut oil, can also be added to colors to make them behave in novel ways. Add oils sparingly, as some may disperse the color so much that it loses pigmentation, or may interfere with color adherence.

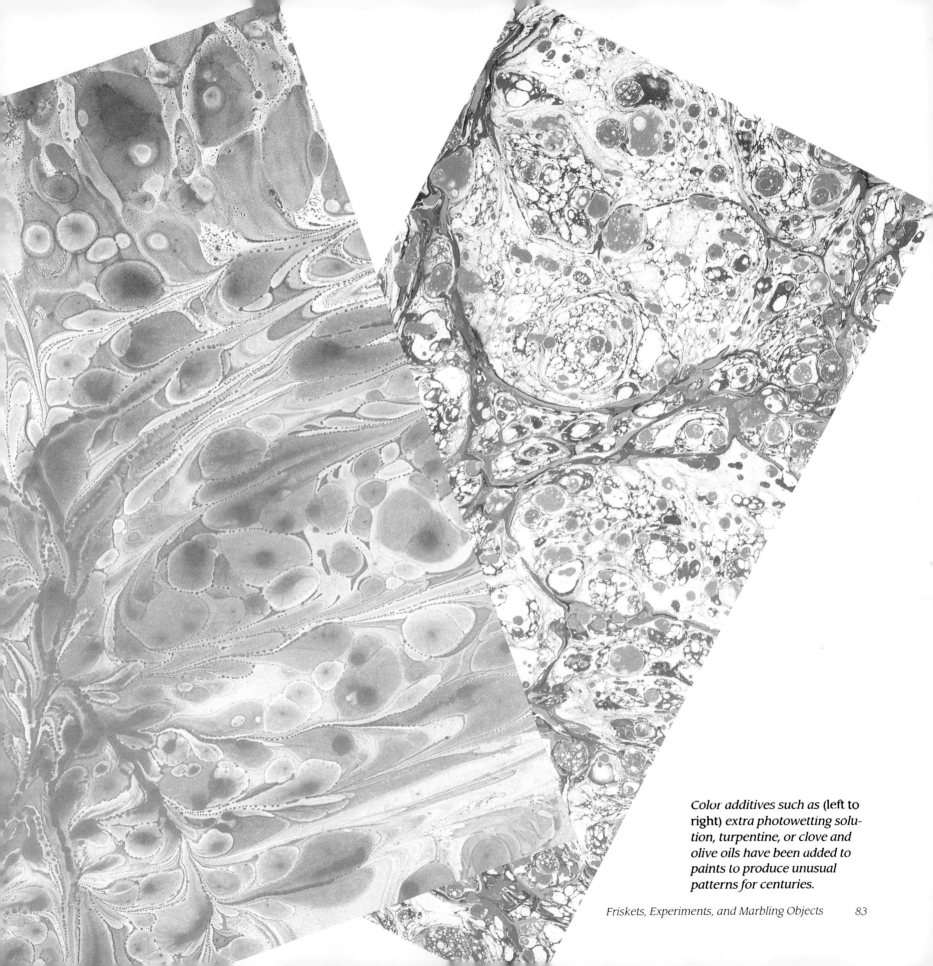

Color additives such as (left to right) extra photowetting solution, turpentine, or clove and olive oils have been added to paints to produce unusual patterns for centuries.

Mixing Coloring Agents

Different types of paints and inks can be mixed together before marbling to create colors with unusual properties. Different paints and inks can also be applied separately to the size and combed together to produce innovative designs. Experiment by mixing any of the following combinations:
- oil paints and watercolor paints
- gouache colors and translucent drawing inks
- metallic oil paints and small amounts of marbling oil colors
- Holbein iridescent gouache colors and marbling watercolors

You might also try marbling with the following, either alone or with other colors:
- colored lacquers (especially effective with oil colors)
- casein paints
- acrylic polymers
- Kiwi Scuff Magic™ shoe polish
- fabric paints

Remember to alum nonabsorbent papers if watercolor paints or water-based inks are used in a combination print. If color sinkage becomes excessive, use dispersant.

Drawing on the Size

(for watercolor marbling only)

Size that is extremely thick or thin will alter patterning considerably. Overly diluted or very old size can become so thin that the wake created by combing will influence images as much as the patterning movements themselves. Conversely, thick size, the consistency of heavy cream, is so reluctant to wander that you can draw or letter on it.

Adjusting the colors for thick size may be a bit difficult at first, as you'll need to add enough dispersant to keep the colors from sinking, but not so much as to cause them to spread out of the configuration you want to achieve. Sometimes spraying the size with gall water before applying color, and working with paints that are extra thick, will make the colors cooperate.

To draw on the size, apply one or more colors to a feather or to a tapered brush until the paint begins to drip. Then, working rapidly so as not to deposit too much color in one area, make the design on the size.

If you plan to letter or to do a representational drawing on the size, remember that the print you create will be a mirror image of what you see in the marbling tray. One way to create designs that print "right-side-out" is to plan the design on translucent paper, turn the paper over, and draw the inverted image on the size.

Because a thick size is relatively stationary, you can do simple drawings on it (below).

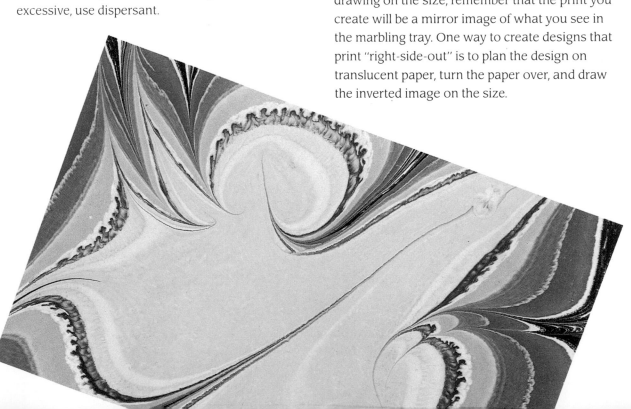

Making a Ghost Print

Often the paint that remains in the tray after a print has been made is dark enough to be used for a second print. This second print or "ghost image" of the first, will resemble the primary print in color only. The action of lifting the first paper will repattern the colors. The ghost print and the primary print on the right are both examples of freestyle ink marbling.

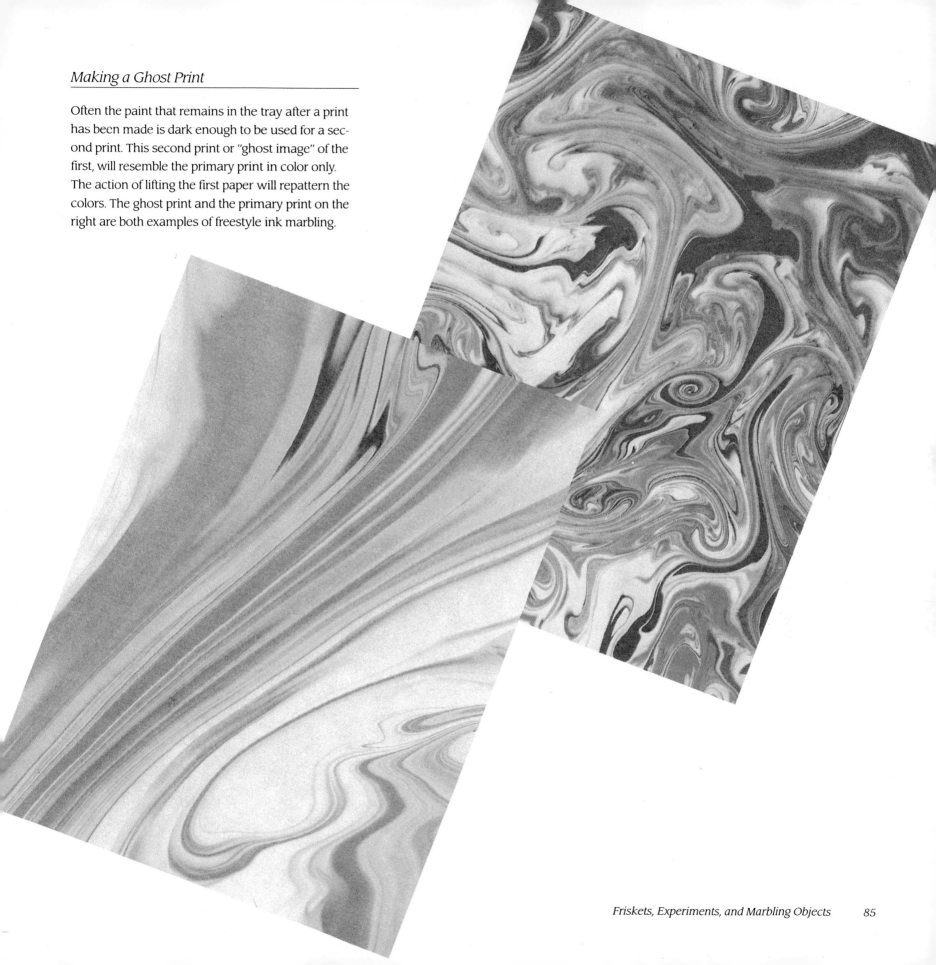

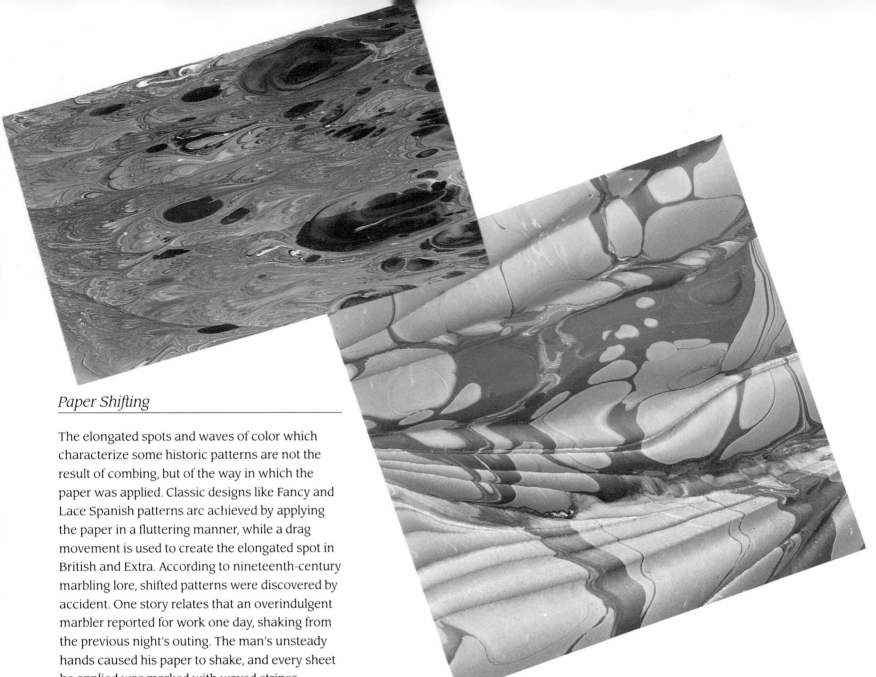

Paper Shifting

The elongated spots and waves of color which characterize some historic patterns are not the result of combing, but of the way in which the paper was applied. Classic designs like Fancy and Lace Spanish patterns are achieved by applying the paper in a fluttering manner, while a drag movement is used to create the elongated spot in British and Extra. According to nineteenth-century marbling lore, shifted patterns were discovered by accident. One story relates that an overindulgent marbler reported for work one day, shaking from the previous night's outing. The man's unsteady hands caused his paper to shake, and every sheet he applied was marked with waved stripes. According to the tale, when the master of the shop was called to view the ruined sheets, instead of chastising the marbler, the master complimented him on the new patterns he'd created.

To make shifted patterns, apply and comb your colors as usual, and then forget everything you've learned about applying the paper correctly. Use quivering, flopping, and sliding movements as you gradually lay the paper down to produce designs like those illustrated on these pages. Devise your own movements, but be consistent in your actions

and try to keep your shifting tight and repetitive. Overly aggressive, gross movements producing a wake may cause excessive color sinkage or push color aside, causing streaks and flashes of paper to appear instead of bands of color. For movements that involve dragging the paper, or moving it from side to side, work with a small enough sheet to allow maneuvering room in the tray. Using a thicker size may help you to produce more regular shifted patterns.

Distorted, elongated patterns and undulating rolls of color are the rewards of shifting.

Tilting the Tray

Although tilting the marbling tray may sound like a rather far-fetched experiment, there is historic precedent for this, too. Some say that tray rocking led to the discovery of shifted patterns and that there was no shaky marbler, but a clumsy one. (Perhaps there were two tipsy marblers working together.) At any rate, during the nineteenth century, marblers would routinely get under their marbling troughs and rock them to set up waves for producing specific kinds of work. We recommend tilting the tray—gently—to alter both combed patterns and uncombed colors.

Placing two large dowels under the center of the marbling tray, and then rolling the tray back and forth, will also give interesting wave effects to patterned and unpatterned colors.

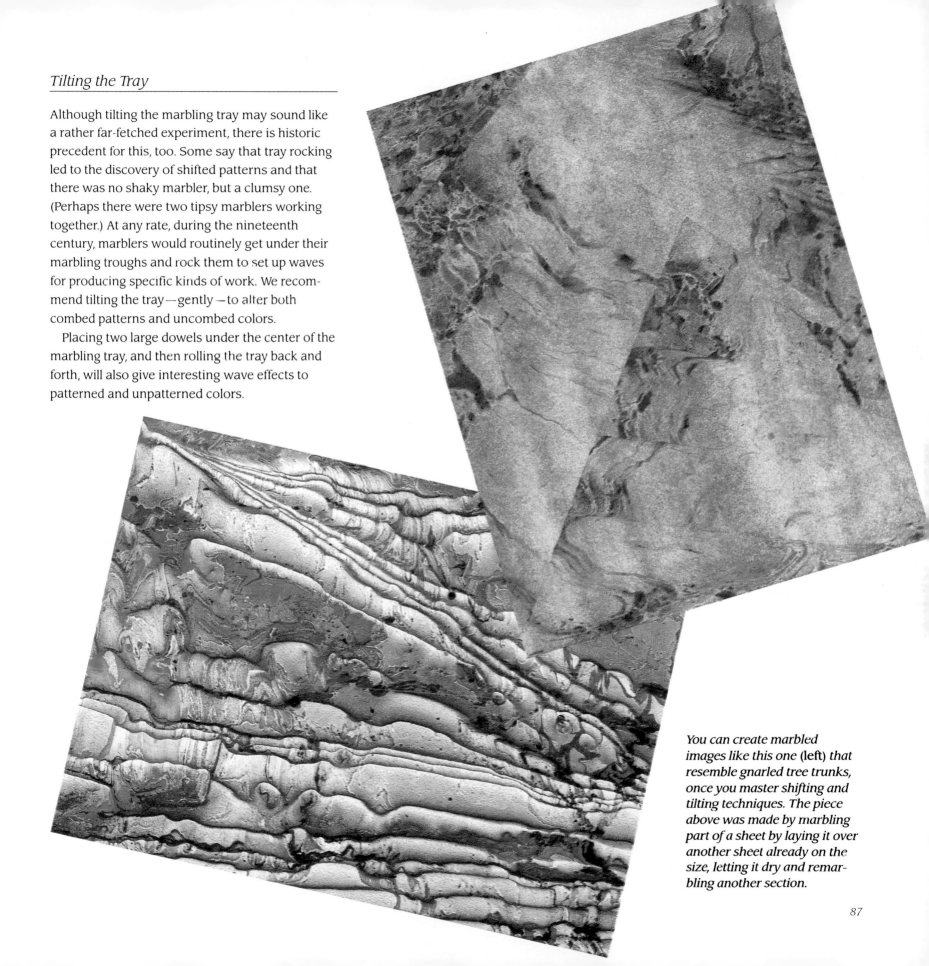

You can create marbled images like this one (left) that resemble gnarled tree trunks, once you master shifting and tilting techniques. The piece above was made by marbling part of a sheet by laying it over another sheet already on the size, letting it dry and remarbling another section.

Marbling With Unskimmed or Partially Skimmed Size

A skin on the marbling size causes color to break up when it's applied or combed. The thicker the skin, the more pronounced the color fragmentation. Images achieved with unskimmed size will be unpredictable, but often quite remarkable.

Incomplete skimming when an excess of color is applied can also yield some interesting images. The backwash of an incomplete skimming of drawing inks yielded the eerie background of Paper Moon, on this page. I wasn't attempting this kind of image, and I remember being a little annoyed that my initial skimming went so poorly, until I really stopped and looked at what was happening in the tray. I decided to print it, and later was quite happy for the detour.

Marbling With Hot or Freezing Size

Extreme variations in the temperature of the size will often make colors behave erratically. Hot size can cause oil colors in particular to mix with one another in veiny patterns. The images are fleeting, however, and you must work quickly to capture them. Watercolors applied to a near-freezing size break up into crystal-like designs.

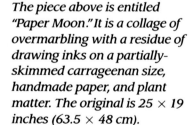
The piece above is entitled "Paper Moon." It is a collage of overmarbling with a residue of drawing inks on a partially-skimmed carrageenan size, handmade paper, and plant matter. The original is 25 × 19 inches (63.5 × 48 cm).

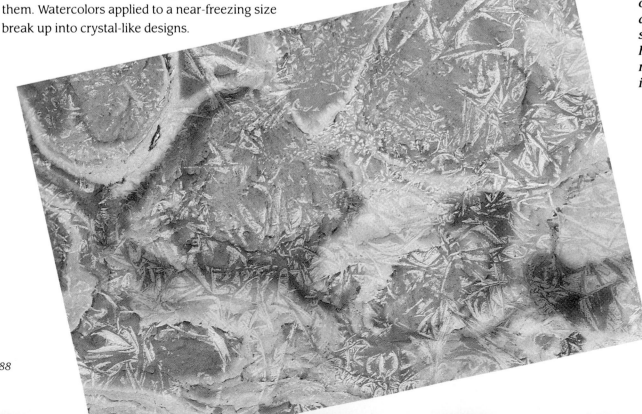

Overmarbling

Overmarbling, or marbling over an already-marbled paper, can be a carefully planned method of creating prints with intricate double images, or it can be a spontaneous means of obliterating unsuccessful marbled designs. Don't discard any of your marbled papers, as the most homely of the lot will often serve as the perfect underpainting for another print.

Papers to be overmarbled with watercolors must be alumed before they're printed. If the base prints are also watercolor, care must be taken to avoid smearing the prints during the aluming process. Don't wipe alum on watercolor prints; blot it on instead, or dip the papers in a tray of alum water and hang them until they're almost dry before flattening them in the alum stack.

When planning overmarbled prints, consider the background and the foreground of the final pattern. Color contrasts, opposing pattern directions, and monochromatic marbled patterns can all be used as design elements. Invisible color (achieved through the use of gall water) can be applied directly to the size in order to allow areas of the original print to show through, or it can be mixed with color to create a translucent film that can be patterned to integrate with initial designs.

Get-gel patterns going in opposing directions and spots of color teased to complement a primary image help make these multiple-image prints successful.

Marbling Objects

Almost anything that will fit in the tray can be marbled. Since huge trays can be improvised by stretching sheets of plastic over a wooden frame, the possibilities abound. At the First International Marbler's Gathering, in 1989, a group of marblers working together managed to oil marble a piece of fabric measuring 18' × 48' (5m × 14m)! Sneakers are often marbled in our workshops. In one of Paul's more memorable classes, a woman marbled the entire front of her dress while helping an equally exuberant elderly friend to marble her cane!

Oil colors and acrylics adhere most readily to objects, but with proper aluming, objects can be marbled with watercolors and inks, as well. Alum may be sprayed on objects if necessary, or applied with a sponge.

Wood, Pottery, Slate, and Three-Dimensional Objects

Fine-grained hardwoods, and softer woods that have been coated with a sealer, will accept detailed marbling. Sealed woods should be scoured with fine steel-wool before marbling (or before aluming and marbling, if you're not using oil paints) to texture them slightly.

To marble a piece of wood, hold it close to the size in a parallel position. Let one edge of the wood make contact with the color before slowly tipping the rest of the wood onto the marbled pattern. Then rinse the wood and let it dry slowly.

Round or curved objects can be rolled onto the marbled pattern or submerged in a container of color and size. Work slowly; if your movements create a wake in the size, the color will be pushed aside.

Bisque-fired or clay pottery, slate, and stone will also accept marbled images. If you're using water-colors, spray or sponge alum on the materials to be marbled, and seal the surfaces with an acrylic spray after marbling to protect the images.

Leather

Smooth leather can be marbled, but suede usually produces an unsatisfactory image. Alum the leather if you're not using oil paints, and handle it as you would fabric or paper. Coating dry leather with a silicone spray after marbling will help preserve the image.

A detail of moulding from a marbled door mirror by Milena Hughes. This mixed-media piece is 52 × 15 inches (132 × 38 cm).

Book Edges

The tradition of marbling book edges began centuries ago. Although primarily a decorative device, the custom had practical applications, as well. Soil that collected on the edges of frequently consulted books, such as dictionaries and encyclopedias, was less visible if the edges of the books were marbled. Record books were also edge-marbled, to discourage people from tampering with them, if any pages were removed from the ledger, the theft would be evident in the interrupted marbled pattern. Marbling was usually done before the book was cased or given a cover, and the top and bottom edges of the book were sometimes marbled along with the fore edge.

Before marbling the fore edge of a bound book, lift the covers out of the way and clamp the pages of the book together by pressing them between two boards held with C-clamps. Scour the clamped edge lightly with fine steel-wool to remove any dirt or oil, and apply alum (if using watercolors) by spraying it on a sponge and blotting the sponge against the fore edge.

Marble by touching the edge of the book to the combed pattern, and then rinse by spraying the clamped edge with water. (Omit rinsing if the pattern looks clean.) Keep the book clamped until the fore edge is dry, and then fan the book pages to separate them.

Glass, Mirror, and Plastic Objects

Smooth materials such as glass, mirror, and plastic will have to be slightly roughened to enable them to accept an alum mordant. To prepare them for aluming, scour them with fine steel-wool, apply several coats of mat fixative, or treat them with an etching spray. Handle smooth materials the same way you handle wood, making sure to seal them after marbling to protect the images.

Envelopes

Envelopes should be alumed before marbling, unless you're using oil paints, but don't place envelopes in the alum stack, as their gummed flaps will stick to other papers. Instead, open the flaps and lay the envelopes aside until they're dry enough to be marbled.

To marble an envelope, hold it parallel to the size surface and slowly tip it onto the color. Rinse and dry the envelope with the flap open.

The light color that remains in the tray after a sheet of paper has been marbled can be used for marbling a few envelopes, or a number of envelopes (manila as well as letter size) can be marbled simultaneously in a tray in which fresh color has been applied. To decorate envelopes with marbled borders or with bands of color, overlap the envelopes when you place them in the tray; that way an area of each envelope will remain clear for addressing. Dilute colors or add gall water to them to create entirely patterned envelopes light enough to be addressed in standard ink, or to create vivid patterns which can be lettered over with light-colored opaque inks.

Use pastel colors or the residue of color from a previous print to create envelopes light enough to address in standard ink. Dark patterns can be lettered in white or silver ink. If you apply colors with a dropper you can leave an unmarbled corridor between them and create a blank area for an address.

A Gallery of Marbling Artists

The face of marbling is changing as more and more contemporary artists adopt marbling as one of their primary mediums. There are still exquisite papers being produced for the book arts, but a lot of unique work is being created that transcends craft. Adventures in composition, color, and texture are a major focus for these marblers. There are several more American marblers whose work deserves to be shown here as well as a number of European, Asian, and Turkish marblers who produce exceptional and innovative images. I would have included many more were it not for space restrictions.

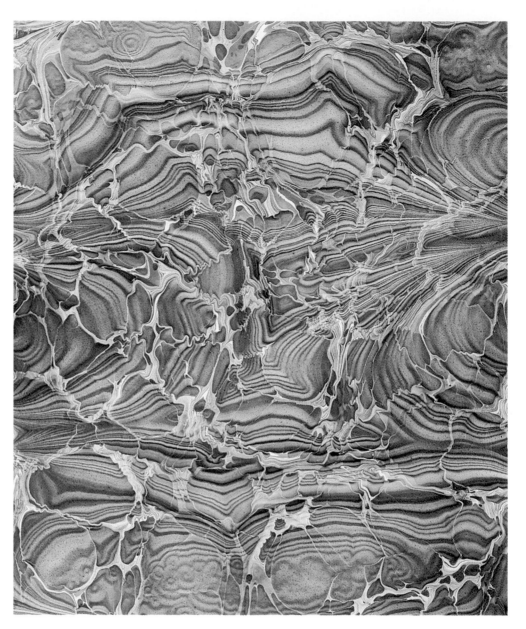

"Moss Agate" by Wendy Addison. Made with oil paints on a cornstarch size. Paint additives and paper manipulation create the unusual effects. Original is 24 × 18 inches (60 × 45 cm).

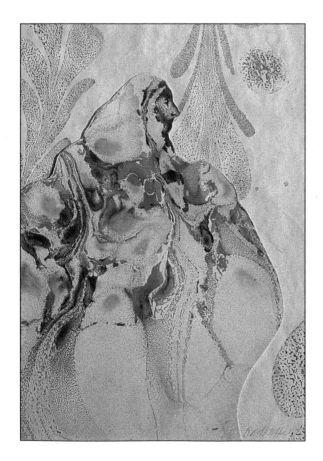

"Queen" by Kay Radcliffe. Made with oil color marbling, drawing, and cut paper. From the collection of Charles Venable Minor. The original is 10 × 8 inches (25 × 20 cm).

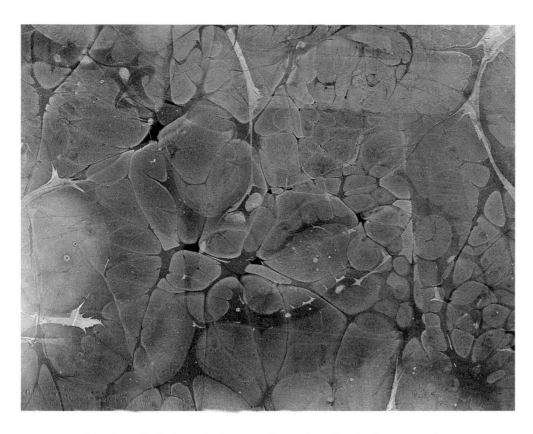

"Pre Petroglyph" by Polly Fox. One in a series of multiple-image prints using acrylics and fabric paints on a carrageenan size, on Japanese paper. The original is 16 × 21 inches (40 × 54 cm).

"Chaco Doorways" by Milena Hughes. Made with acrylic marbling and ink on paper, 36 × 24 inches (90 × 60 cm).

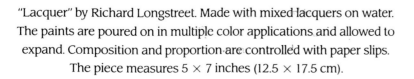

"Lacquer" by Richard Longstreet. Made with mixed lacquers on water. The paints are poured on in multiple color applications and allowed to expand. Composition and proportion are controlled with paper slips. The piece measures 5 × 7 inches (12.5 × 17.5 cm).

"Seven Point Two" by Jennifer Philippoff Tosh. Multiple-image sumina-gashi marbling on Japanese paper with Boku Undo dyes. The original is $9^{1}/_{2} \times 14^{1}/_{2}$ inches (24×36 cm).

"Flame Dance" by Eileen Canning. Watercolor marbling on a carrageenan size, on Beckett Antique paper with a quadruple mat. One in a series of explorations into the essence of heat and fire. The original is 28 × 22.5 inches (70 × 57 cm)

"Birds" by Pamela Smith. A multiple-image piece; the first color application was done with a stencil, the second with a methyl cellulose resist, and a third color was applied over these. Acrylic gouache on a carrageenan size, on Rives paper. The original is 24 × 18 inches (60 × 45 cm).

Chapter Eight
Paper Projects

SOMETIMES A SHEET OF MARBLED PAPER IS SO UNIQUE, OR PRESENTS SUCH
a powerful image, that the thought of cutting it or using it in a project seems
like a violation of the marbling craft. We call such papers "monoprints" and sometimes
frame them to enjoy as paintings. The majority of prints, however, don't fall
into this category. Special papers may be set aside for consideration, but after they lie
in state for a few days, they usually get buried in a growing stack of
favorites. After a few weeks at the tray, even novice marblers begin to wonder what
to do with all the prints they've created. ⁂ The answer to the dilemma
is to start a marbled paper business, or to put the papers to use—either as
decorative elements combined with other crafts, or as the primary
focus—in any number of paper projects.

A variety of boxes and books covered with oil and watercolor
paper. Wooden tubes with brass endcaps can be made into
earrings or used as a novel box handle.

The textures and patterns of your papers may suggest uses to you: thin suminagashi papers for origami, heavy construction or cover stock for unusual postcards, a Feather pattern for covering a goose-quill box, or a Nonpareil design for lining an antique steamer trunk.

The projects that follow are designed to give you a glimpse of the many ways marbled papers can be used, and to teach you enough about working with paper to pursue ideas of your own.

Paper Projects
- The Paper Folio
- Cards and Envelopes
- Bookmarks and Jewelry
- The Covered Lampshade

Paper and Chipboard Projects
- The Accordion Book
- The Picture Mat
- The Memo Book

Equipment

Square. A squaring device, such as a T-square, or a carpenter's square or triangle, is needed to assure that paper corners are cut at right angles and that edges are perfectly straight. A steel square is ideal, as it can be used for measuring and squaring corners and can also provide a guiding edge for cutting tools.

Metal Ruler. If you don't have a steel square, a metal ruler is necessary for measuring and cutting.

Cutting Tools. A mat knife or an X-Acto* knife is the fastest and most accurate tool to use for cutting straight lines, while a compass cutter is the most efficient tool for cutting circular shapes. A sharp pair of scissors, although less desirable, can be used to cut paper but will not divide chipboard.

Cutting Board. A piece of glass (with sharp edges taped), or a self-healing cutting mat protects the tabletop when cutting with a knife.

Pressing Boards. Two boards and a few heavy books or bricks can be used as a makeshift book press to protect glued projects from warping as they dry. The boards should be smooth and flat.

Compass. A compass is needed for drawing circular shapes in several projects. If possible, purchase the type that accepts a blade as well as a drawing lead.

Pencil. A sharp, soft #2 pencil is best for drawing light erasable lines. Hard pencils sometimes leave an indentation in papers.

Glue Jar. The glue used in projects should be kept in a small jar. Baby-food size is fine.

Toothpicks. Toothpicks are useful for applying glue to hard-to-reach places where a brush would be too big to use safely.

Sponge. A dampened sponge is handy for removing glue from fingers before it gets transferred to marbled papers.

Burnisher. A bookbinder's folder is the best tool to use for folding and creasing papers, as well as for smoothing glued surfaces. A tongue depressor, a smooth letter opener, or the spine of a plastic comb can be used as a substitute burnishing tool.

Scoring Tool. An awl, a darning needle, or a tapestry needle is needed for scoring thick papers before they're folded.

Paper Punch. A punch is needed for making ribbon-tie holes in some projects.

Materials

Spray Fixative. To prevent chalking, coat all water-color marbled papers with an acrylic spray fixative before using them in projects.

Marbled Paper. The projects call for marbled papers of various weights. Cover-weight, text-weight, and bond-weight papers can all be used.

Plain Paper. Cover-weight and text-weight unmarbled papers are used along with marbled sheets in some of the projects.

Scrap Paper. Sheets of newsprint or of other inexpensive paper are placed under the paper being glued, and are discarded immediately after use.

Waxed Paper. Waxed paper, which is used to cover glued areas during pressing, prevents wet marbled sheets from staining other parts of the project or from sticking to the pressing boards.

Tracing Paper. A sheet of tracing paper is placed between the burnishing tool and the damp glued paper to prevent the paper from being damaged during burnishing.

Glue. Sobo™ glue, Elmer's™ glue, or "Yes"™ paste can be used to glue projects. "Yes" paste has the added benefit of not wrinkling even thin papers. Rubber cement is not recommended, as it tends to eventually bleed through papers and discolor them.

Ribbon. Ribbon of various thicknesses is called for in several projects.

Chipboard. Binder's board or chipboard, approximately 1/16" (2 mm) thick, is used as cover material in paper-and-chipboard projects.

(Additional materials needed will be noted at the beginning of each set of project instructions.)

Procedures

The following procedures will be referred to throughout the chapter. Practice them on scrap paper and board to familiarize yourself with them before attempting them on projects.

Finding Paper Grain. Paper and chipboard, like fabric and wood, have what is known as a "grain," or fiber direction. A paper folded with the grain will crease easily and lie flat, while one folded against the grain will be difficult to crease and won't hold its shape as well. Wet papers tend to curl with the grain, so make sure that when you glue papers to boards, the grain of both materials is running vertically, parallel to the height of the project. If materials with opposing grain directions are glued together, they'll pull against each other as they dry, and the tug-of-war will evidence itself in a warped finished project.

To test for the grain direction of a sheet of paper, take the sheet and bend it in half. If the paper bends easily, offers little resistance, and collapses on itself, you're bending with the grain. If the paper fights back, you're bending across the grain.

To test for the grain direction of a sheet of chipboard, hold the long edges of the sheet in your hands, so that the length of it stretches out in front of you, and attempt to bend the sheet. Little resistance means the grain is running parallel to your forearms. Considerable resistance means it's running crosswise.

Draw an arrow indicating grain direction on the sheet of chipboard; this will help you to avoid losing track of the grain direction as the board is cut and changes shape.

Scoring. Heavy papers are difficult to crease unless they're scored—which means using a pointed instrument to scratch or indent the paper surface—before they're folded. To score, hold a metal rule firmly on the fold line of the paper. Then, using the rule as a guide, drag the point of an awl or heavy needle down the fold line. Apply just enough pressure to break the surface of the paper. Cutting too deeply into the paper will weaken it, and the process of folding and unfolding it, as in an accordion book, will eventually cause the weakened paper to tear.

Cutting. Make sure that the blade of your tool is sharp when cutting materials with a mat knife or an X-Acto® knife. Dull blades require a great deal of pressure to accomplish a job and will sometimes rip papers instead of cutting them cleanly. Hold the knife in an upright position and slide it against a metal rule as you cut; tilting the blade will produce an undesirable beveled cut. A single pass with a sharp knife will cut through most papers. Chipboard, however, will be more difficult to cut. Don't attempt to cut chipboard in a single stroke; the pressure required will cause you to slant the knife. Instead, cut it in several strokes, holding the guide rule firmly in place along the cutting track until you have cut cleanly through the board.

Gluing. Thin glue or "Yes" paste is less likely to wrinkle papers and can be spread more rapidly than a thick adhesive. Speed is necessary to prevent one section of the paper from drying while you're working on another section. Brush the glue on rapidly but carefully; glue that's haphazardly applied will cause paper to adhere in some places and not in others. Work over a piece of scrap paper when applying the adhesive, and starting at the center and working toward the edges, spread the glue evenly over the entire surface of the paper or chipboard. Apply only as much glue as necessary to bond the materials—wet papers tend to stretch, and overly glued sheets will be difficult to burnish properly.

Burnishing. Smoothing or burnishing glued papers helps bond them, pushes out wrinkles, and eliminates air bubbles that may be trapped between wet papers and the materials they cover. To avoid damaging the paper that is to be burnished, cover it with a sheet of tracing tissue. Work from the center of the glued paper outward in order to smooth and flatten it.

Pressing. Papers that have been stretched by gluing will shrink as the glue dries, and they tend to warp the boards to which they've been bonded. To prevent any curling or warping, place projects in a press immediately after they're finished, and keep them perfectly flat until all materials are dry. A simple press can be made from two smooth boards and several heavy books or bricks. Place waxed paper above and below the project in order to protect it, then sandwich it between the boards, evenly distributing the books or bricks over the top board. The amount of glue and the thickness of the materials used in the project will determine how long a project should be pressed; leave it under the weights overnight to be on the safe side.

Working With Adhesive Release Paper. An alternative to gluing, if you're only planning to do a few projects and find the traditional bookbinding techniques difficult, is to use an adhesive release paper such as PMA (positional mounting adhesive), made by 3M. This paper consists of a thin, double-sided adhesive sheet sandwiched between two protective papers. To use it, you peel away one protective paper and apply that adhesive side to the wrong side of your marbled paper. When you peel away the other protective paper, you're left with a sticky sheet of marbling that's ready to be burnished onto bookboards, lampshades, or other materials. The drawbacks are that adhesive release papers are rather expensive, and projects made using some release papers may not last as long as those made using glue.

Paper Projects

The Paper Folio

Loose papers, photographs, or samples of marbled prints can be kept in a decorative paper folio. To make the folio pictured, which holds a 5″- (12.7-cm-) square set of paper samples, you'll need a heavy sheet of marbled paper approximately 13″ (33 cm) square. Commercial cover stock, or quality papers such as Canson or Strathmore, can be used for the project.

Begin by drawing a rectangle 6″ × 12″ (15 cm × 30 cm) in the center of a sheet of marbled paper as shown below. (Pencil your lines lightly on the wrong side of the paper, as you'll want to erase them later.) Make small dots on the 3″ (7.6 cm), 6″ (15-cm), and 9″ (23-cm) marks of each 12″ (30-cm) line. Positioning the point of the compass at

The paper folio with marbled paper samples enclosed.

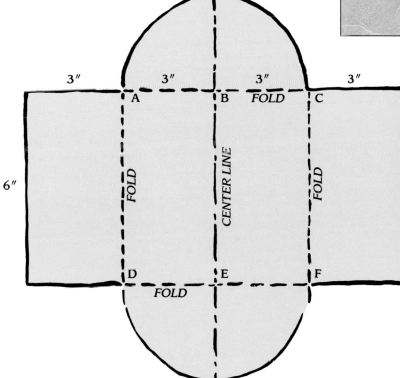

one 6″ (15-cm) mark (B), extend the tool so the pencil (or blade) of the compass lands on point C. Then swing the compass to draw an arc from C to A, forming one folio flap. Starting at point E, make another arc from D to F to form the second flap. Cut out the folio, erase your pencil lines, and score and fold all flaps along the lines indicated. Finally, punch holes in the curved exterior flaps to make a ribbon tie.

Marbled papers of various weights can be used to create cards and envelopes. Panels of thinner marbled paper can be applied to purchased stock, or stiff paper can be cut into squares and rectangles and folded in half to form standing cards. Paper can also be folded a quarter of the way in from either edge, as shown below, to produce a gate fold that opens to reveal a marbled

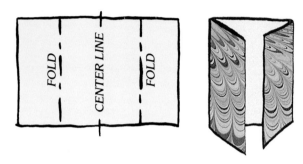

center or, if the marbled side is on the outside, a clear space for a message or a photograph. Thinner papers can be used if they're folded in half lengthwise and folded again in the opposite direction to create a quarto, or French-fold, card.

Handmade cards can be decorated by gluing cutout shapes or ribbon to them, or by cutting windows into the cards to reveal other papers, foils, or photographs that are glued behind the opening.

The decoration can be done in the marbling tray, too; fantasy marbled designs, for example, can be created especially for card use.

Purchased envelopes can be marbled to coordinate with card designs, or if you prefer, marbled paper can be made into envelopes. To make your own envelopes, use an existing envelope as a template. Choose a purchased envelope of the appropriate size, steam open the glued flaps, and open out the envelope to produce a flat pattern. Trace around the perimeter of the envelope onto a sheet of marbled paper, cut out the shape, fold on the proper lines, and apply glue to three flap edges, leaving the fourth open. Then burnish the envelope and press it until it dries.

Bookmarks and Paper Jewelry

In addition to being used for making gift tags, scraps of marbled paper left over from larger projects can be used to make bookmarks and paper jewelry. Strips of marbled paper can be mounted alone, or side-by-side with cover stock to create striped patterns. Ribbon can be added as a design element, or it can be looped through a hole punched at the top of the bookmark to form a traditional page-marking device. Heavy marbled sheets can be laminated with clear adhesive film to make more durable bookmarks, with the added benefit that clear film intensifies your marbled colors. Punching holes in a plain cover paper and mounting it over a strip of marbled paper to allow circular windows of marbling to show through can also be used as a design device.

Paper jewelry can be cut from laminated stock in a variety of shapes. To create unique pins, small pieces of marbled paper and shiny stars made from mylar or foil can be applied to pieces of colored mat board. Thin mat board, marbled and cut into triangles, can be glued together in various combinations and attached to pin and earring backings, as well. Miniature collage pins and earrings can be made by applying layers of different marbled papers to small pieces of mat board. Jewelry made with mat board should be varnished to protect it from moisture. To make lightweight paper earrings, tiny origami birds or accordion-folded fans can be spray varnished and attached to earring wires.

The Covered Lampshade

A marbled-paper lampshade can make an attractive focal point in a room. Illuminated at night, the shade casts a charming glow and assumes a different character than it does during the day.

Thin papers can be used to allow a maximum of light to shine through the marbled pattern, while heavy, opaque papers can be used to help create a special mood in a room. The color and pattern of the shade to be covered will influence the success of the project. If lampshades with existing designs are covered with marbled paper, the original patterns may show through the marbled ones when the lamp is lit. This may sound interesting, but unless they're planned, double patterns rarely work together. White translucent shades are recommended for the project. Light-colored shades can also be used, but they'll alter the color of the marbled paper when the lamp is on.

A drum lampshade has parallel sides and an equal diameter on top and bottom, so it can be neatly covered with a rectangular sheet of marbled paper.

A parchment hexagonal shade such as the one shown can be covered by measuring one section, making a pattern out of heavy acetate, and tracing around it to cut the six marbled panels. The clear acetate will allow you to view the section of marbled paper you're cutting; this is a particular help if you're trying to match a marbled pattern around the shade. Alternating marble patterns or colors from section to section can sometimes create an interesting effect. The bars separating the panels may be covered with ribbon or contrasting paper, if desired.

Covering a tapered shade is difficult and requires something close to surveying skills to accomplish. The easiest way to cover a tapered shade is to find an inexpensive type of shade, buy two, and dismantle one to use as a pattern.

The procedures followed in the lampshade projects can be used to cover other forms, too. For instance, a juice can can be transformed into a marbled pencil-holder (the pencils çan be covered with marbled paper, too), or into a vase for dried flowers. Stiff cardboard tubes can be given a bottom and covered to hold toothpicks or fireplace matches; an old oval letter-holder can be refurbished to become part of a matching desk set.

A deep teal cover stock paper was marbled for this shade to complement the brass base.

Paper-and-Chipboard Projects

These projects incorporate some of the principles of simple bookbinding. With a little practice, you'll become skillful enough to measure and cut papers and chipboard so that they're square and without ragged edges. Despite the fact that chipboard is covered with marbled paper in these projects, any imperfections in the preparation of the board will be visible in your finished product. Matching the grain of paper with that of the board, and following correct gluing, burnishing, and pressing procedures will also be important to the success of your work.

Another procedure, that of mitering corners, should be understood and practiced before projects are attempted.

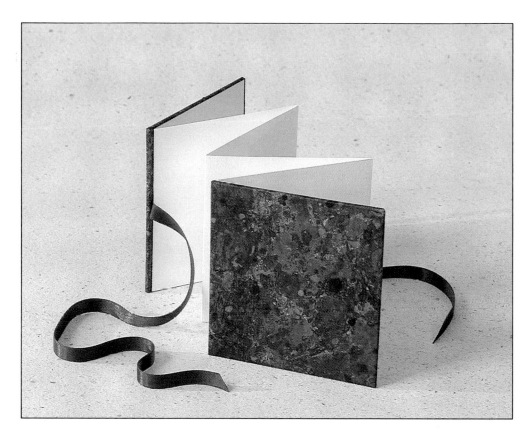

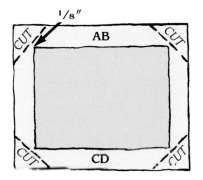 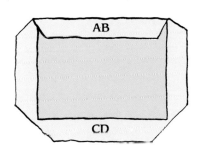 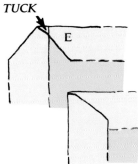

The ability to make tight, well mitered corners is the mark of a good craftsperson. Loose book edges can ruin an otherwise beautiful project.

Mitering Corners. Mitering refers to the way papers are folded, fitted together at the corners of the boards they cover, and glued down. Begin mitering by cutting off the corners of the marbled papers, as shown (above), leaving a space approximately 1/8" (3 mm) between the edge of the board and the end of the paper. Glue and fold flap A-B (above right), and repeat the cutting and folding procedures at corners C and D. The small overlap of paper (E) visible in the closeup drawing (right) appears when the top and bottom flaps of

paper are folded down and is the result of leaving the 1/8" (3-mm) space between the paper and the board. This overlap prevents the corner of the chipboard from showing when the side flaps of paper are folded in. Tuck these overlaps in toward the side flaps at each corner before folding and gluing down the side flaps.

If you have difficulty positioning the glued flaps because your paper is thick, you may find that prefolding flaps and corners before applying glue will make the job easier.

A design of Eastern origin, the accordion book is composed of a long sheet of folded paper enclosed between two covers. Both sides of the paper can be used to hold photographs, haiku poems, marbled papers, pressed flowers, or other mementos. If the folded paper is fairly stiff, the open book can be arranged to stand for display. To make a small accordion book like the 3¾″ × 4¼″ (9.5-cm × 10.8-cm) one on the previous page, you'll need light- to medium-weight marbled paper, some chipboard, and some plain cover-weight paper for the folded pages. Make the covers for the accordion book as follows:

After determining the size of the cover boards you wish to cut, transfer the measurements to a sheet of chipboard or similar material, and making sure that the grain of the board runs vertically, use a mat knife and square to cut your two cover boards. Check to see that the boards match, that the corners are cut at right angles, and that the edges are straight. Then prepare the paper covers.

Position your marbled paper so that the grain direction matches that of the cover boards, then cut two pieces of paper 1″ (2.5 cm) longer and 1″ (2.5 cm) wider than the pieces of chipboard. Place each board in the center of the back of a marbled sheet so that it's surrounded by a ½″ (1.3-cm) paper margin. Then trace around the corners of each board to make positioning marks indicating where to place each board when you glue it down.

Prepare to glue the front cover-board by setting the marbled paper aside and placing a sheet of scrap paper beneath the chipboard. Then brush one side of the board with glue and place it glue-side-down within the positioning marks on the marbled sheet. Discard the scrap paper and wipe any glue from your fingers before turning the marbled paper right-side-up and burnishing it to the cover board. When you're satisfied that air bubbles and wrinkles have been smoothed out, turn the paper over so that the chipboard is again facing you. Working over a clean sheet of scrap paper, proceed to miter the corners of the marbled paper, gluing the paper flaps to the chipboard.

Repeat the procedures to paper the back cover-board. Then press both boards overnight to make sure they don't warp as the glue dries.

While the covers are being pressed, you can make the accordion-folded pages:

To determine the height of the pages, measure the height of the cover and subtract ¼″ (6 mm) to allow for ⅛″ (3-mm) margins around the end-papers when they're glued to the book covers. Likewise, the width of the folded pages is determined by measuring the width of the book cover and subtracting ¼″ (6 mm) to allow for margins. For the book shown on page 105, each page will be 4″ (10.2 cm) high and 3½″ (8.9 cm) wide.

Using a mat knife and a rule, cut a long strip of stiff cover-weight paper to use for the pages of the book. The width of the paper should correspond to the height of the pages. (If you're making the book shown, the strip will be 4″ (10.2 cm) wide.) The length of the paper, which determines how many pages the book has, can be extended after the accordion folding has begun. Cut several strips of paper to join together later if you require a book with numerous pages.

Because an accordion fold book has no case binding, there's no limit to the number of pages it can have. If you want to display both the front and the back of each page, however, it's a good idea to extend the joining fold to span the width of the page it meets before gluing it down.

GLUE

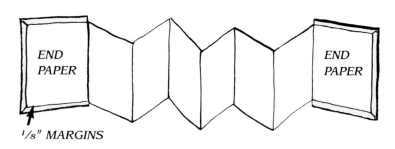

END PAPER

END PAPER

⅛″ MARGINS

Prepare to fold the strip of paper by measuring off one page width and drawing a faint line to mark where the first fold will be. If you're working with heavy paper, as suggested, you'll also want to score the paper on this line. Then fold the first page of the book. Continue by turning the paper over, scoring if necessary, and making another fold away from you. Keep turning the paper over, and continue accordion folding until you reach the end of the strip of paper. Cut off any excess that's not wide enough to include as a page, or that folds in the wrong direction to use as an endpaper. If you want to increase the number of pages in your book, join similarly folded pages together as illustrated (far left).

Apply the endpapers to the cover boards by brushing glue on the papers and positioning them so that a ¹/₈" (3-mm) margin surrounds them as shown (near left). Burnish the papers down. Then place a sheet of waxed paper between the covers and the first pages of the book in order to prevent any glue from penetrating, and press the books overnight.

After you've made a few simple books, you may want to try making some with decorative cut-out covers. You'll need a compass cutter to create a circular window, but a rectangular window can be cut with a mat knife and a little patience.

Quilled paper or an accordion-folded fan could be used to decorate the books or a number of other objects, such as a Chinese coin, a pressed flower, or even a birthday candle, could be placed in the window to embellish the cover or to establish a theme for the book.

Covered Picture Mats

Larger boards with cut-out windows may also be covered with marbled paper and used as mats for picture frames. You can glue the marbled paper to the board before cutting the window and merely fold it back as shown (right). Mats that have already been cut are available in a variety of sizes and may also be covered. Pale, subtle papers often harmonize well with color photographs or botanical prints, while bolder patterns can complement drawings or calligraphy.

Large covered boards can be glued to expanding files to transform them into decorative desk accessories. Ribbon ties may be added by gluing them between the papered boards and the file.

Covered boards can also be used to transform metal bookends, while smaller papered boards can be covered with clear adhesive paper to create a set of coasters.

Covered picture mats can be made to match the colors and theme of the photos they hold. The miniature folio in the foreground holds a tiny shell from the Scottish coast where this photo of my daughter Jennifer was taken.

The Memo Book

A marbled case-binding can provide a lasting cover for a notepad. Kept by the telephone, it's an attractive way of making sure that paper and pencil are always at hand. The case can be designed to coordinate with other paper-covered objects, such as a marbled stamp-box or pencil-box, to become one of several matching desk accessories. The 4½″ × 6½″ (11.4-cm × 16.5-cm) memo book pictured was designed to hold a standard 4″ × 6″ (10.2-cm × 15.2-cm) pad of paper and still leave room at the top of the pad to insert a pencil. Memo pads come in various sizes; make a cover to fit the size you prefer.

Begin the project by cutting matching cover boards and a chipboard spine that's ½″ (1.3 cm) high and the same width as the covers as shown (below left). Lay a sheet of marbled paper wrong-side-up on your working surface, and position the boards on the paper, as shown, making sure that the edges of the boards line up accurately with one another. Allow at least ½″ (1.3-cm) border on three sides of each cover, and a ⅛″ (3-mm) space between the spine and each of the cover boards. (This space is called the "hinge" of the case.) Draw positioning marks for all three parts of the cover,

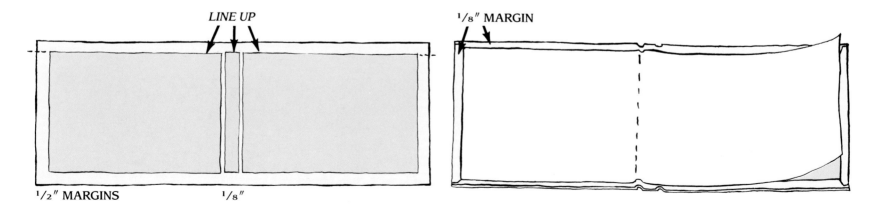

trim the marbled paper border to an even ¹/₂″ (1.3-cm), turn over and begin gluing the boards down, onc at a time, as follows.

Coat one cover board with glue, place it in position on the marbled paper, turn the paper right-side-up, and burnish it until it's smooth. Then glue and burnish down the spine and the second cover board. Miter the corners of the cover paper and fold down the paper flaps, then press the opened case for about an hour.

Cut a marbled paper lining for the case; it should be ¹/₈″ (3 mm) shorter than the cover on all four sides. Then place the lining in position on the case and make faint pencil dots to help you maintain equal margins when you glue it down. Once you're more experienced, you won't need these dots, but for a novice, getting the glued liner down correctly can be quite a challenge.

The next step is to coat the entire back of the paper liner with glue and begin attaching it to the case. Position the left-hand side of the lining on the left cover board, and press part of it down with your hand so that it won't slip. Then, brushing the paper toward the right, work the liner into the hinge groove, as shown. Rub the liner onto the spine and into the second hinge groove before lowering and brushing the rest of the paper onto the back cover. Burnish the liner onto the case until all areas are smooth.

Continue burnishing by closing the case over the notepad (or over any other support that's approximately ³/₈″, or 1-cm, thick) and *very gently* creasing the cover paper into the hinge grooves. The wet paper will tear easily, so use the side of your finger or a cloth-covered burnishing tool for this operation.

Press the closed, supported case overnight, making sure that the spine and hinges of the case extend beyond the pressing boards so they're not crushed by the weight.

Once the case has been pressed, glue a wide strip of oaktag, or a similar heavy paper, to the lining of the back cover; this will hold the notepad backing in place.

The projects here represent a few of the many ways to enjoy your marbled papers. Fabrics, of course, could also be used on some of the projects if applied with mounting adhesive. A trip to your local library can no doubt offer additional inspiration. Some of the subjects you might investigate include decoupage, hand bookbinding, origami, mask making, collage, paper sculpture, jewelry making, and kite construction. Architecture, too, might be a topic to pursue. I've always hoped to find time to build a marbled castle. A closetful of various-sized cardboard tubes will one day take the form of towers and parapets marbled in a "stone" pattern. Suminagashi paper, of course, will line the moat.

With some marbling experience and some simple binding skills, you can create any number of marbled treasures.

Chapter Nine
Constructing Marbling Equipment

THE FOLLOWING DIAGRAMS EXPLAIN HOW TO BUILD PROFESSIONAL MARBLING equipment. A number of liberties may be taken with the directions. For instance, oak, redwood, or Plexiglas can be substituted for less expensive building materials, and tooth placement on combs and rakes can be modified to achieve looser or tighter marbled patterns. The overall size of the equipment can also be changed. The 20″ × 30″ (51-cm × 76-cm) marbling tray suggested is small and light enough to be manageable, yet large enough to accommodate many standard-sized papers. If you're interested in pursuing miniature work, or in marbling oversized papers, however, the tray may not suit your needs. Experiment until you find the right one.

Making an assortment of combs and rakes with varying tooth-spacing will allow you to increase your repertoire of marbled images.

Alter the dimensions of the tray to fit your marbling requirements, making sure that the modified tray, minus the drain area, is slightly larger than a standard paper size. Otherwise, you may have to trim larger sheets to fit the tray, or work with smaller papers than desired. Patterning tools are scaled to fit the 20″ × 30″ (51-cm × 76-cm) tray; adjust them proportionately to fit larger or smaller trays.

In order to protect the wooden parts of marbling equipment from repeated water exposure, cover them with several coats of waterproof varnish before use. Comb teeth, tool hooks, and other metal parts of equipment not covered by varnish should be made from brass or stainless steel to prohibit rusting.

Painting the bottom of your tray white is also something to consider; this will make the floating colors easier to see.

Marbling Tray, Rinse Board, and Skimming Board

The material used for these pieces should be lightweight and rigid, such as ¹/₂″ (1.3-cm) exterior plywood or synthetic siding. These instructions are for a tray 20″ × 30″ (51 cm × 76 cm):

1) Cut the following:
   - 1 piece 20″ × 30″ (51 cm × 76 cm) (base)
   - 1 piece 20″ × 30″ (51 cm × 76 cm) (cover and rinse board)
   - 2 pieces 2″ × 30″ (5 cm × 76 cm) (long sides)
   - 2 pieces 2″ × 19″ (5 cm × 48 cm) (short sides)
   - 1 piece 2″ × 19″ (5 cm × 48 cm), with one long edge cut at a 45-degree angle (drain partition)
   - 1 piece 2″ × 19″ (5 cm × 48 cm) (skimming board)
2) Drill a ³/₄″ (1.9-cm) drain hole in one corner of the base.
3) Fill gaps in the wood with a wood filler, and sand smooth.

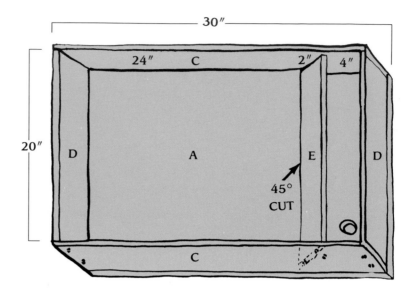

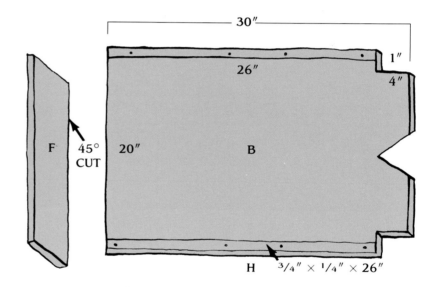

4) Glue together the edges of the tray and drain board, and clamp to dry.
5) Bead all wood joints with additional glue.
6) Reinforce the tray corners, the bottom, the edges of the drain partition, and the rinse board edge-strips, with screws.
7) Sand the tray, rinse board, and skimming board, and apply three coats of urethane or waterproof varnish.
8) Insert a 2″ (5-cm) piece of rubber tubing in the drain hole; this will help control splashing.

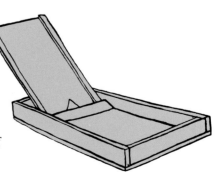

Wooden Rake

1) Cut the following:
   - 1 strip of pine $\frac{1}{2}$" × $1\frac{1}{2}$" × 24" (1.3 cm × 3.8 cm × 61 cm)
   - 12 pieces of $\frac{3}{8}$" (1-cm) dowel, each $3\frac{1}{2}$" (8.9 cm) long
2) Sand all of the pieces smooth.
3) Drill $\frac{3}{8}$" (1-cm) holes at 2" (5-cm) intervals along the length of the strip of pine.
4) Sharpen one end of each of the dowels in a pencil sharpener.
5) Coat the blunt ends of the dowels with wood glue and insert them into the holes.

Note: The spacing and thickness of the dowels can be varied to achieve whatever effect you desire.

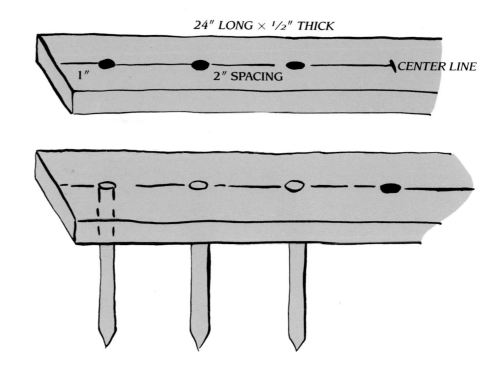

24" LONG × $\frac{1}{2}$" THICK

1"   2" SPACING   CENTER LINE

T-pin Comb

1) Cut 2 strips of pine $\frac{1}{4}$" × 1" x 18" (.6 cm × 2.5 cm × 46 cm).
2) Sand the strips smooth.
3) Apply a line of wood glue to strip A (one section at a time).
4) Set $1\frac{3}{4}$" (4.4-cm) T-pins in the glue, using strip B to support them.
5) Apply a second line of glue over the pin heads, and allow the glue to dry.
6) Glue strip B on top of strip A, and clamp to dry.

Note: Use the above procedure to make another comb, 22" (56 cm) long, to pattern in a horizontal direction.

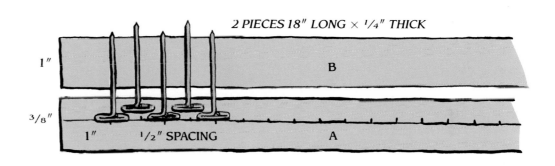

2 PIECES 18" LONG × $\frac{1}{4}$" THICK

1"   B

$\frac{3}{8}$"   1" $\frac{1}{2}$" SPACING   A

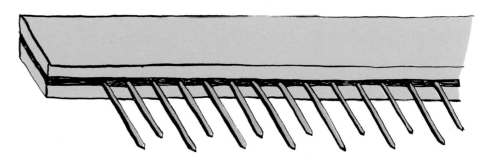

2 PIECES 18" LONG × ¹/₄" THICK

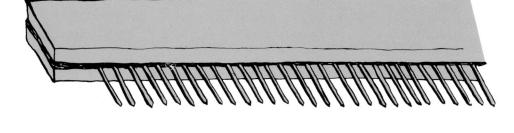

³/₁₆"

1"   ³/₁₆" SPACING

Follow the procedure for making a T-pin comb, but use long dressmaker pins and set them ³/₁₆" (5 mm) apart.

Tool Rack

1) Cut 1 strip of pine or decorative molding ¹/₂" × 2" × 26" (1.3 cm × 5 cm × 66 cm).
2) Sand the strip smooth.
3) Drill a small hole 1" (2.5-cm) in from each end of the strip; these will be used to hang the rack.
4) Screw 1 ³/₈" (3.5-cm) square bend hooks into the strip to hold your patterning tools and skimming board. Vary the spacing of the hooks to accommodate different-sized tools.
5) Screw medium screw-eyes into the ends of tools to allow for easy hanging on the hooks.
6) Use screws to attach the rack to a wall or table.

Freestyle Comb

1) Cut 2 strips of pine ¹/₄" × 1" x 6" (.6 cm × 2.5 cm × 15 cm).
2) Sand the strips smooth.
3) Apply a line of glue to one of the strips, and set T-pins ¹/₂" (1.3 cm) apart along the length of the strip.
4) Assemble according to the directions for a T-pin comb.
5) Cut the clothespin handle as indicated.
6) Glue the handle to the center of the comb.

CUT →

1¹/₄"

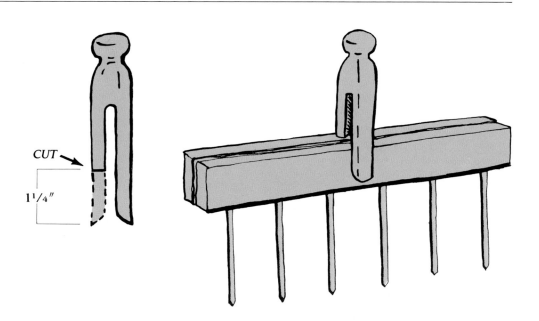

Bouquet Comb

1) Cut 1 strip of pine $1/4'' \times 1^1/2'' \times 17''$ (.6 cm × 3.8 cm × 43 cm). (An identical strip of wood should also be cut if a comb cap is desired.)
2) Sand the strips smooth.
3) Drill two staggered rows of $1/16''$ (2-mm) holes 1" (25 mm) apart along the length of the strip of pine.
4) Insert and glue the T-pins. (Place a dot of glue where they pierce the comb base.)
5) Add the comb cap, if desired.

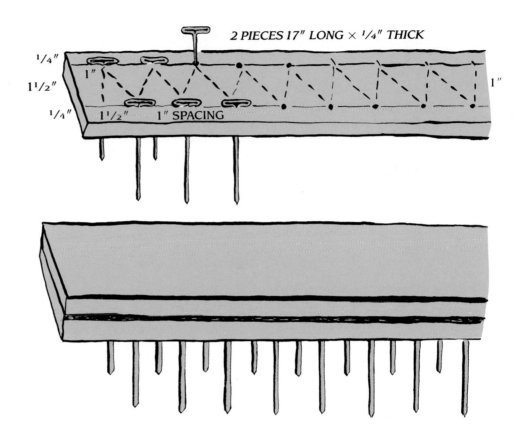

2 PIECES 17" LONG × 1/4" THICK

1/4"

1"

1¹/₂"

1/4"   1¹/₂"   1" SPACING

1"

Pegboard Bouquet Comb

1) Cut 1 strip of $1/8''$ (3-mm) pegboard 17" (43 cm) long and 2 holes wide.
2) Cut and sharpen enough $1/8''$ (3-mm) dowels to fill half of the holes in the pegboard.
3) Apply glue, and insert the dowels in the pegboard holes as shown, to form two staggered rows of teeth.

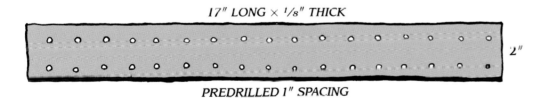

17" LONG × 1/8" THICK

2"

PREDRILLED 1" SPACING

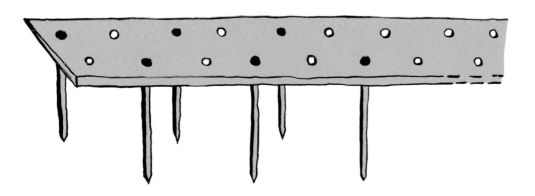

Further Reading

On Marbling

Easton, Phoebe Jane. *Marbling A History and a Bibliography.* Los Angeles: Dawson's Bookshop, 1983.

Fox, Polly. *Marbling on Fabric.* Taos: Fresh Ink Press, 1989.

Guyot, Don. *Suminagashi: An Introduction to Japanese Marbling.* Seattle: Brass Galley Press, 1988.

Halfer, Joseph. *The Progress of the Marbling Art.* Buffalo: American Bookbinding Co., 1894. (Reprinted: Fresh Ink Press, 1989.)

Loring, Rosamond B. *Decorated Book Papers.* Cambridge: Harvard University Press, 1952.

Maurer, Diane and Paul. *An Introduction to Carrageenan and Watercolor Marbling.* Centre Hall, PA: Diane Vogel Maurer, 1984.

Maurer-Mathison, Diane. *Decorative Paper.* New York: Mallard Books, 1993.

Nevins, Iris. *Traditional Marbling.* Sussex, NJ: Iris Nevins, 1986.

Nevins, Iris. *Fabric Marbling.* Sussex, NJ: Iris Nevins, 1989.

Nicholson, James B. *A Manual of the Art of Bookbinding.* Philadelphia: Henry Baird, 1856. (Reprinted: Garling Publishing Co., 1980; Iris Nevins, 1985.)

Weiss, Franz. *The Art of Marbling* (translated from the German with samples by Richard J. Wolfe). North Hills, PA: Bird and Bull Press, 1980.

Woolnough, C.W. *The Art of Marbling.* London: A. Heyalin, 1853.

Articles by and about marblers appear in *Ink and Gall* Marbling Journal, PO Box 1469, Taos, NM 87571.

On Bookbinding and Papercraft

Hollander, Annette. *Bookcraft: How to Construct Notepad Covers, Boxes and Other Useful Items.* New York: Van Nostrand, 1974.

Ikegami, Kojiro. *Japanese Bookbinding.* New York: John Weatherhill Inc., 1986.

Johnson, Pauline. *Creative Bookbinding.* Seattle: University of Washington Press, 1963.

Miura, Kerstin Tini. *My World of Bibliophile Binding.* Berkeley: University of California Press, 1984.

Shannon, Faith. *Paper Pleasures.* New York: Weidenfeld & Nicholson, 1987.

Supply Sources

Amsterdam Art
1013 University Avenue
Berkeley, CA 94710
(415) 548-9663
• Papers; oil, gouache, acrylic marbling
  paints

Andrews-Nelson-Whitehead
31–10 48th Avenue
Long Island City, NY 11101
(718) 937-7100
• Papers; board

Basic Crafts Co.
1201 Broadway
New York, NY 10001
(212) 679-3516
• Bookbinding supplies; oil and watercolor
  marbling supplies

Boku-Undo USA, Inc.
594 Broadway, Suite 1003
New York, NY 10012
(212) 226-0988
• Suminagashi marbling supplies

Brooks & Flynn
Box 2639
Rohnert Park, CA 94927-2639
(800) 822-2372
• Everything for fabric marbling, including
  pre-scoured fabric samples

Cerulean Blue, Ltd.
Box 21168
Seattle, WA 98111-3168
(206) 443-7744
• Fabric and suminagashi marbling supplies

Colophon Book Arts Supply
3046 Hogum Bay Road SE
Olympia, WA 98506
(206) 459-2940
• Bookbinding supplies; watercolor and
  suminagashi marbling supplies

Creative Fibers
5416 Penn Avenue South
Minneapolis, MN 55419
(612) 927-8307
• Fabric marbling supplies; air brush paints

Curry's Art Store
756 Yonge Street
Toronto, ON M4Y 2B9
(416) 967-6666
• Papers; art supplies

Daniel Smith Inc.
4130 First Avenue South
Seattle, WA 98134
(800) 426-6740
• Oil, acrylic, gouache, and sumi paints;
  brushes; papers; binding supplies

Davey Board Co.
164 Laidlow Avenue
Jersey City, NJ 07306
(201) 653-0606
• Binder's board

Decorative Papers
Box 749
Easthampton, MA 01027
(413) 527-6103
• Watercolor and acrylic marbling
  and supplies

Diane Maurer, Hand Marbled Papers
Box 78
Spring Mills, PA 16875
(814) 422-8651
• Watercolor and suminagashi marbling
  supplies; books on marbling and papercraft

Grafix
344 Queen Street W
Toronto, ON M5V 2A2
(416) 593-5888
• Papers; art supplies

Kakali Hand Made Papers
1249 Cartwright Street
Granville Island
Vancouver, BC V6H 3R7
(604) 682-5274
• Papers; art supplies

New York Central Supply Co.
62 Third Avenue
New York, NY 10003
(212) 473-7705
• Watercolor, oil, and acrylic marbling
  supplies

Paper-Ya
9&10 1666 Johnston Street
The Netloft
Granville Island
Vancouver, BC V6K 3S2
(604) 684-2531
• Papers; art supplies

Sam Flax
111 8th Avenue
New York, NY 10011
(212) 620-3060
• Papers; board; oil and acrylic marbling
  supplies

Stephen Kinsella, Inc.
Box 6863
Brentwood, MO 63144
(314) 644-1270
• Papers

Textile Resources
10591 Bloomfield
Los Alamitos, CA 90720
(213) 431-9611
• Fabric and acrylic marbling supplies

Thai Silks
252 State Street
Los Altos, CA 94022
(800) 722-SILK
• Silk yardage; silk scarves

Index

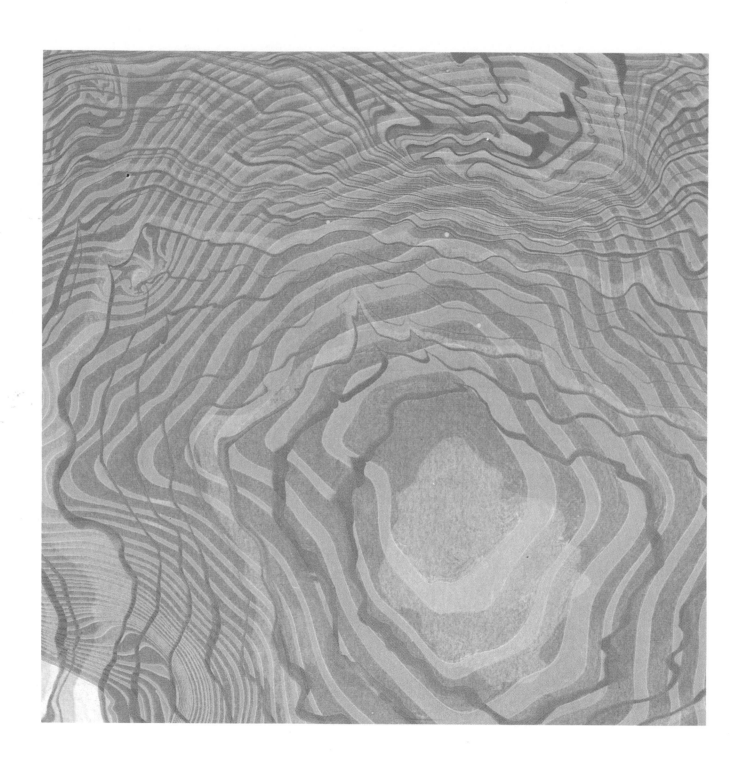